CW00556329

How to Be Strategic

'A must-read for everyone who ever deals with complex, important challenges. There are many take-away gems here that will help you push through the knotty centre of hard-to-resolve problems. Highly recommended!' Richard Rumelt, Harry and Elsa Kunin Emeritus Professor of Business & Society at Anderson School of Management, UCLA and author of *Good Strategy, Bad Strategy*

'Being strategic is best accomplished when you develop the right thinking skills, mindset and toolset to help you work smarter. Fred has distilled an entire career's worth of expertize and experience into a comprehensive, concise and practical guide that will enable anyone, in any situation, to develop their strategic thinking' Tiffani Bova, Chief Growth Evangelist, Salesforce and *Wall Street Journal* bestselling author of *Growth IQ*

'Bold new thinking and innovation is hard. This book gives a wonderful and inspirational look into wide-ranging frameworks and theories to spark new thinking and strategy' Tom Goodwin, author of *Digital Darwinism* and Head of Futures and Insight at Publicis Groupe

'Practical and comprehensive, *How to Be Strategic* reveals how to build your strategic mindset and gives you the most powerful tools' Roeland Assenberg, Director, Strategy and Banking, Monitor Deloitte Netherlands

ABOUT THE AUTHOR

Based in London and working globally, Fred Pelard is a **strategy trainer, consultant, facilitator and coach**. He specializes in helping teams and organizations solve strategic problems. A French rocket-scientist by training, he's been lecturing on strategic thinking and complex problem solving to the CEOs and management teams of major corporations and consulting firms around the world for the best part of 20 years. **He makes smart people smarter.**

Fred started his career in management consulting with Deloitte, completed his MBA at INSEAD, and has worked as a strategist ever since. First with Kalchas (a medium-sized Bain and McKinsey spin-off, eventually sold to CSC) and then with Instigate Group, where he works with some of the leading organizations in media, retail, consumer goods, financial services, industry and consulting. He currently divides his time between three areas of equal interest and excitement:

- designing and delivering **strategic thinking sessions** (training, talks, etc.)

- facilitating **strategic away-days** for boards and management teams

- conducting **high-impact strategy projects** and ideas generation challenges.

Typical interventions include 90-minute talks for up to 500 people, two-day senior-level workshops with up to 50 executives, and five-day intensive sprint-venturing innovation sessions with participants from across the company. Footprint is truly global, from San Francisco to Shanghai, Stockholm to South Africa, and all points of the compass in between (live, and via Zoom, Webex, etc.)

Selected repeat clients include Allianz, Barclays, BBC, Betfair, Booz Allen, Channel 4, Deloitte, Expedia, HSBC, IKEA, John Lewis, Johnson & Johnson, London Business School, OC&C Strategy, Sainsbury's, Thomson Reuters.

Check out Fred's website and YouTube channel to get a sense of what he teaches.

www.fredpelard.com

www.youtube.com/fredpelard

HOW TO BE STRATEGIC

FRED PELARD

BUSINESS

PENGUIN BUSINESS

UK | USA | Canada | Ireland | Australia
India | New Zealand | South Africa

Penguin Business is part of the Penguin Random House group of companies
whose addresses can be found at global.penguinrandomhouse.com.

Penguin
Random House
UK

First published 2020

001

Copyright © Fred Pelard, 2020

The moral right of the author has been asserted

Typeset by Jouve (UK), Milton Keynes

Printed and bound in Great Britain by Clays Ltd, Elcograf S.p.A.

A CIP catalogue record for this book is available from the British Library

ISBN: 978–0–241–42303–5

Follow us on LinkedIn: https://www.linkedin.com/company/penguin-connect/

www.greenpenguin.co.uk

MIX
Paper from
responsible sources
FSC™ C018179

Penguin Books is committed to a sustainable
future for our business, our readers and our
planet. This book is made from paper certified
by the Forest Stewardship Council.

To the quest

CONTENTS

PART FOUR
HOW TO GET THE BEST SOLUTION APPROVED ('PUSH')

PART FIVE
HOW TO KEEP IMPROVING AS A STRATEGIC THINKER ('AGAIN')

INTRODUCTION

Hard work, talent, contacts, luck. These are important for success in life. Whatever your chosen pursuit. In business, one also needs to add one more ingredient: the ability to be strategic. Smart work, if you will.

Being strategic is a skill, and it can be learned. I've been teaching it for the last 20 years, to over 10,000 executives across 60+ organizations. Superior strategic thinking skills boil down to two things: a specific mindset (to tackle the uncertainty of the future, where all strategic issues reside) and a wide toolset (to craft credible solutions out of very little actual data). This book contains five parts. The first and last parts focus on the mindset, and the middle three on the toolset.

> - How to **Solve Complex Problems** ('Think')
> - How to **Generate Great Ideas Quickly** ('Up')
> - How to **Eliminate Options in No Time** ('Down')
> - How to **Get the Best Solution Approved** ('Push')
> - How to **Keep Improving as a Strategic Thinker** ('Again')

'Think' introduces the markedly different ways in which different people deal with Complexity. This part explains the expert, analytical, creative and strategic approaches to complex problem solving, and how each approach relies on a different mix of data, structure and brilliance. 'Think' concludes with the Rollercoaster of Strategic Thinking as the ultimate mental model for working smarter, not harder, and Up-Down-Push as the practical way to achieve that.

'Up' focuses on three structured techniques for generating great ideas quickly. Like a camel in the desert, each technique takes you quite far on very little water (aka data). Asking, respectively: 'What would need to be true to achieve the success we seek?', 'How well are we currently meeting customers' needs and expectations?' and, 'What more successful versions of our business lie on the edge of our consciousness?' 'Up' takes you quickly to a place of Clarity on any strategic issue.

'Down' brings to bear three analytical techniques for eliminating many options in no time. Checking, respectively, that: an idea is better than all the other ideas you can think of in the future; it can be proven to work as a prototype in the present; and available past data broadly agrees with the conclusions of present and future testing. 'Down' takes you methodically to a place of Certainty over time on any strategic issue.

'Push' combines three packaging techniques for getting your preferred solution approved. These techniques include guidelines for, respectively: verbalizing your answer in memorable, plain English; putting dollar estimates around it; and crafting a compelling story. 'Push' takes your stakeholders (boss, clients, colleagues, etc.) to a point of Conviction, where they agree to your strategic recommendation.

Rollercoaster
of Strategic Thinking

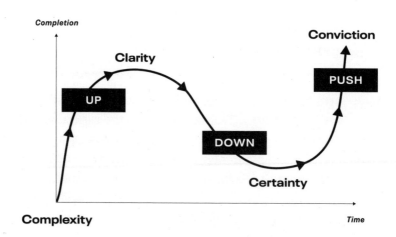

'Again' offers lifetime tips to help you keep improving as a strategic thinker. Slogans such as 'Vote First, Then Debate', 'Small Teams Go

Faster', 'The Third Solution Is Often the Best' are explained further, instilling a highly practical roadmap to navigate the next 10 years of your career. 'Again' takes you to a place of deep personal Confidence in your ability to welcome any future strategic challenge with a smile, and to solve it.

Each page in this book will help you become more strategic by the day. With clear structure, memorable visuals, concrete examples and simple principles. Up–Down–Push. Up–Down–Push. Whatever the strategic issues you're facing. *How to Be Strategic* is a combination of the best techniques I've ever come across, distilled into a simple programme to support your learning and development. Keep on reading – and work smarter. Don't worry, be strategic.

PART ONE

HOW TO SOLVE COMPLEX PROBLEMS ('THINK')

FOUR ROUTES TO COMPLETION

How can I be more strategic? **The hallmark of a successful executive, entrepreneur or freelancer is the ability to be more strategic than one's peers or competitors.** Not just the ability to manage well the day-to-day operational issues, but having a better feel for the future. Finding a way through the uncertainty towards the best long-term solution for you, your team, your clients or your whole company.

Being strategic is a skill. Like sudoku, taking selfies or flossing your teeth. Some people are born great at it. Others, like me and you, can learn the techniques and become good at it quite quickly, and better over time. At its core, being strategic is a mindset. It's a way to solve problems. It's not about how many years of experience you've got, or how well you can crunch numbers on Excel. It's not even about how high your IQ is, or how many business theories you know. It's just about the way you think about problems. So, let's talk about the way you think.

On most problem-solving activities, particularly in business, a stakeholder (client, boss, etc.) gives you an amount of time to reach completion on a particular problem. We can therefore plot most problem-solving activities on a map, where the horizontal axis captures the time it takes to solve a problem, and the vertical axis measures the percentage to completion. Every problem on this map starts life in the bottom left corner and ends up in the top right corner, fully completed over the time allowed. The bottom left corner of our map is the Complexity corner. Before you start your project, the stakeholder who asked you to help (your boss, your client, etc.) is not sure of the answer. They find the issue complex, and they need a bit of help. They've asked you to spend time coming up with one answer that they are happy with at the end. The top right corner of the map is the Conviction corner. At that point, at the end of the time frame you've been given, your stakeholder expects 100 per cent completion, in the shape of one answer that they are convinced by.

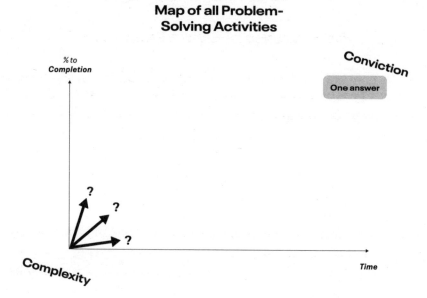

Map of all Problem-Solving Activities

A good way to think about problem solving is this: an activity that takes a group of people, over time, on a journey from Complexity to Conviction. You'll realize shortly that there are four very different ways to travel from the Complexity corner to the Conviction corner:

> the Staircase of Expert Execution
> the Submarine of Analytical Research
> the Helicopter of Creative Discovery, and
> the Rollercoaster of Strategic Thinking.

Each route follows a very different path on our map. All routes start in the bottom left (Complexity corner) and all end up in the top right (Conviction corner), but after taking widely different turns. Most people are not aware of these four routes, and as a consequence often fall back on the same approach to problem solving, for all the problems they face.

When you know more Routes to Completion you can crack more problems satisfactorily, and especially the toughest ones. The first step towards becoming more strategic is to think about the way you think, and to recognize your current problem-solving habits and preferences.

The Staircase of Expert Execution

The Staircase of Expert Execution is the approach most of us use **when we don't actually realize that we are solving a problem**. We just execute a solution we already know – or we ask another expert to do so for us.

There are many problems in life for which we already have a pretty good idea of what the end-point answer looks like, even before we start. Lacing up one's shoes, moving house, implementing new HR or supply chain processes, etc.

In a personal context, imagine that you put on a pair of shoes in the morning, and you've got to lace these up. For most of us after the age of five, lacing one's shoes is no longer a problem that requires a lot of complex thinking. We know the final answer right from the start. The time to completion is maybe five seconds, the completion itself is always a pair of perfectly laced shoes, we know exactly how we're going to go about it, and there's a clear progression towards completion over time. We're experts at tying up our shoelaces.

In a business context, imagine that your company is looking to drastically improve a key process – for example, achieve best practice in warehousing, or optimize some HR processes towards perfection. Words like 'optimize', 'best practice', 'perfect' are a clue that there is an expectation that an optimal answer exists out there already. We just need to find the people who've got it, and ask them to help us achieve it.

When this expertise doesn't exist inside the company, we turn to external providers. A good supplier should have a pretty good idea, even at the beginning of the project, of what the optimal answer will look like at the end.

What most firms do is put together a request for proposal, and invite a few potential contractors to bid for the project. You'll typically find three components in each of the bids. First is a list of credentials, with names of satisfied prior clients, and nice words from them. Second is a workplan, or methodology, detailing the steps to be undertaken to arrive at the desired outcome. Third are a few résumés of the key people who will be delivering the project, their expert skills, and where they learned them.

The client is then able to assess each provider on the basis of these credentials, methodologies and résumés. The chosen winner is typically the one that succeeds in convincing the client, even before the project starts, that they know the optimal answer, and can be counted upon to reliably deliver on it. The best expert.

Right at the start of the project, at the Complexity corner, the chosen winner is already able to offer a workplan listing all the tasks to be undertaken to arrive at the desired outcome, including time frame and workload. Which is why the shape of the problem-solving activity on our map looks like a staircase, from the bottom left to the top right.

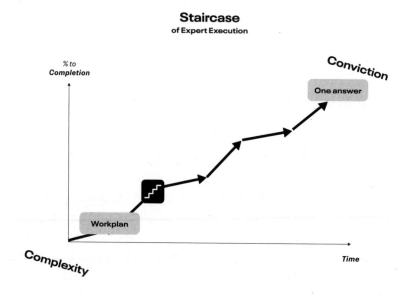

Staircase
of Expert Execution

It's a staircase, and not a straight line, as tasks sometimes happen faster than expected, and sometimes they are slower. If you're the stakeholder, the way you manage your supplier is to check at regular time intervals that the supplier has completed the various tasks they promised they would carry out.

The Staircase of Expert Execution is the path that problem-solving activities follow when done by experts. Any expert. It's the methodical execution of already known tasks, towards completion of an already identified outcome.

Experts solve problems asked of them by comparing the problem at hand to problems they've already tackled. They can identify the component tasks necessary to completion, and weave these together in a workplan from the start. The Staircase route is a brilliant way to solve problems, and it works for lots of problems. You can use the Staircase to plan a house move, or a wedding, upgrade your IT systems, or select a management consulting firm to implement new HR processes, etc.

Arguably, most of us spend most of our days solving most of our problems using the Staircase of Expert Execution. Our CVs and LinkedIn profiles are a public track record of our expertise. They capture the long list of the things we've already done in our professional life, and the problems we now know how to solve using the Staircase. Not every problem you will face in life, however, will be amenable to resolution by an expert, or by the Staircase route. What happens when nobody can credibly contend, at the beginning of the project, that they already know for sure what the optimal answer is?

The Submarine of Analytical Research

Imagine a situation, at the beginning of your project, **where you can't really see what the answer might look like**. You have a big range of possible solutions, and you don't know which one to choose. Or the exact opposite, and you don't even have a clue what the answer might look like. In one scenario you're faced with an overabundance of possible solutions, a dense cloud of possibilities, in the other a complete desert.

You clearly can't build a Staircase to a cloud or a desert, so what do you do instead? Many people go horizontal. They realize that they face lots of unknowns, and choose to spend a fair amount of time turning these unknowns into facts. Undertaking the research, doing the analysis, looking at market trends, benchmarking the competition, talking to customers, etc. Building a comprehensive knowledge base, via one-off research, to compensate for the lack of readily available expertise.

The implicit expectation here is that if you invest time turning those unknowns into facts, researching and gathering more and more data, analysing it smartly, then, at some point, you are going to get a critical mass of facts and information. At that point, somewhat late in the process, like a torpedo shooting out from a hidden submarine, the answer will burst from below the waves and impress upon all the brilliance of your answer and your achievement.

The Submarine of Analytical Research is sometimes referred to as the deductive logic approach to problem solving, and it's a beautiful one.

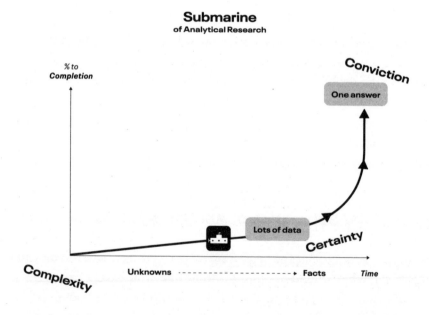

Many of you will recognize this as the approach you've been taught at school or university. Academia loves a Submarine. You invest a huge amount of time, whether it be hours, days, weeks, months or years, slowly coming up with a heavily researched paper that you share just before your deadline.

There are lots of other professions where everyone's fortunes are extremely tied to their ability to employ the Submarine of Analytical Research for problem solving. Can you think of a few such professions? Let me mention lawyers, engineers and accountants. I could add investigative journalists, academics and all sorts of researchers. These professions share a belief system whereby the proper way to solve any problem is to invest the time to find the facts, become familiar with these facts, process them smartly, and then the answer emerges.

The Submarine of Analytical Research is the path that problem-solving activities follow when undertaken by people who believe that you need the facts first, before you can envisage any answer. No data, no solution.

The big benefit of the Submarine route as a problem-solving approach is that you turn lots of unknowns into data, which gives you certainty regarding your eventual answer. The corner of the map we shoot for with this approach, the bottom right corner on our map of problem-solving activities, is the Certainty corner. It's the time and place in your project where you can ground your recommendation in the certainty that comes with having lots of data.

The Submarine of Analytical Research is very powerful and very effective. When it works. It does, however, rely on three significant conditions to work.

The first one is that you need really smart people. There is so much information gathered in the horizontal part of the Submarine route that you need a really good memory to carry all that information around. You also need a fairly agile brain to manipulate all that data to extract the answer in the vertical part of the Submarine route. This is why the Submarine of Analytical Research is commonly used at interview level to discriminate between applicants at university, in corporate jobs, or in consulting. A typical interview in all these pursuits might involve asking the candidate to ingest a large quantity of data quickly (read an article in three minutes, read a business case study in 10 minutes), summarize the salient points cogently at speed, and present a brilliant answer while stressed out and afraid of running out of time.

The second condition for the Submarine route to work is for the data to show up. What if you invest a huge amount of time looking for data, hoping to gather lots of it, and you don't find any? You might say in the twenty-first century it's not the availability of data that is the issue, it's the quality of data. Fair enough. Not always, though, and I'll explain why shortly. First, take a look at the vertical axis on our map, the Completion axis. If you put a dotted line through it halfway up, you'll realize that anything below that dotted line will count as an input. You're quite far away from completion. Anything above that dotted line, however, is more of an output, as you're getting closer to completion.

One thing that is noticeable with the Submarine route is that you invest a lot of time in the issue space, the input space, below the dotted line. You only come up towards the solution space, the output space, above the dotted line, much later than you do with the Staircase route; much more towards the back end of the project.

The Submarine route acknowledges that we don't really know what the answer looks like from the beginning, and so we're going to do a big trade-off. We're going to invest more time doing the research first, and we'll spend longer underwater in the input and issue space, but at the end we'll have a more informed and convincing solution. If the data shows up.

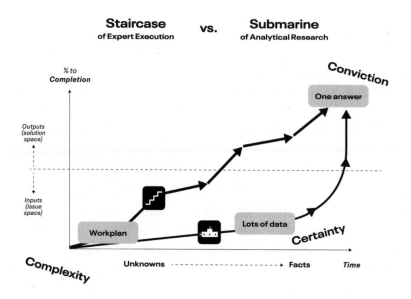

This leads us to the third big issue with the Submarine route: the time frame. Imagine that you've been working on something for a few weeks or a few months, and a new stakeholder arrives. Irrespective of the time frame you were given by the previous stakeholder, one of the first things they'll want to know is your likely draft recommendation for something you've been working on for a while now. If you've been following the Submarine approach all you can say is, 'I've got lots of data, I'm ploughing through more data, but I'm sorry I'm still quite far from an answer.' That may leave your new stakeholder somewhat unimpressed.

Likewise, imagine that one of the digital giants (Amazon, Apple, Google, etc.) has just announced they're buying your most direct competitor. How does that affect the project you're currently working on? Here, too, your stakeholder will probably ask for an answer right away. Ready or not. Data or not. So, there are quite a few drawbacks to the Submarine of Analytical Research: you need smart people to embark upon it; your solution arrives quite late in the process; you might find that there isn't enough quality data available for a solution at all; and you might look silly in front of a senior stakeholder if circumstances lead them to ask you for an answer earlier than you expected.

And yet, the Submarine route, as we've seen earlier, is still the problem-solving approach of choice in many smart professions, including the law, journalism, engineering, accounting, etc. Why is it so? The answer is simple. It boils down to the time horizon of the data that is crucial to each profession.

Between past, present and future, where do lawyers find the facts that are most critical to their work? In the past. If you look for facts in the past, availability of data is never a problem. A lawyer preparing for a day in court will look to the past for precedents on her case. If you find a precedent, that's a great data point, and even if you find no precedent that's still a useful data point.

Where do investigative journalists find their facts? In the past too, with a sprinkling of the present. When investigating the possible link between a foreign power and any politician, you go back several years to gather all the facts you seek. With maybe a few questions asked today of the key participants.

Where do engineers find their facts? In the present. Because engineering operates within the known boundaries of science, if you're conducting an engineering project and you're missing some data, all you need to do is measure. You do an experiment, and you measure things. Engineers can create in the present whatever data they need. There's a clear theme here.

Professions that rely heavily on the Submarine route for problem solving tend also to rely heavily on facts from the past and the present. And where do the key facts of strategic thinking reside? In the future.

Of course, solving strategic issues relies on facts from the past and the present too, but the most critical data you need for resolution does come from the future. And that's why, the more strategic the issue we are trying to solve, the less likely the Submarine of Analytical Research is going to work. The more strategic the problem you are dealing with, the less applicable the Submarine route becomes.

The horizontal route relies heavily for its success on the availability of data, in both quantity and quality. And when you look to the future, which is where most of strategic thinking operates, data is going to be scarce and often highly unreliable. We'll see shortly how the third route to Completion compensates for that.

Before we do, let me alert you to a little irony. The horizontal Submarine of Analytical Research is clearly a smarter approach to problem solving than the diagonal Staircase of Expert Execution. You only get to be an expert once you've put in the years, in your specialist field, and there are only so many things any one of us can ever become an expert at. Whereas, once you're smart enough to cope with the demands of analytical research and processing, you can apply this horizontal approach to pretty much any problem.

So the horizontal, Submarine route is the preferred problem-solving method of smart, analytical people. And strategy and strategic thinking are commonly held to be some of the smartest problems around. Yet the horizontal route doesn't work very well to solve such strategic issues. How ironic. The problem-solving method most beloved of eggheads doesn't work for the most egghead of problems!

That's because it's impossible to solve the future using just hard facts, since there are no hard facts in the future, just hidden possibilities. The future can't be analysed; it can only be created.

The Helicopter of Creative Discovery

The Helicopter of Creative Discovery is the approach you take **when you can't really work out the answer right from the beginning** (no Staircase of Expert Execution available here), and you're clear that **data is going to be sparse and unreliable** (so sub-optimal use of the Submarine of Analytical Research). What do you do next, then? You go vertical.

You accept that you're faced with a bunch of unknowns, and that it's all very chaotic. So you don't waste time trying to turn these unknowns into facts. Instead, you quickly impose some structure on the chaos that surrounds your problem, and you shoot for three or four creative options.

As a rule of thumb, always invest about 5 per cent of the overall time available to you to arrive quickly at that structure with those options. So spend three minutes structuring a number of options if you've been given an hour to undertake a task, spend two hours if you've got a week, etc.

Let's continue exploring the thinking habits and problem-solving preferences of certain professions. You remember we mentioned that lawyers, investigative journalists, engineers, accountants, etc. tend to automatically default to the horizontal Submarine route to solve problems. Because they were selected, trained and rewarded for using that approach.

Can you now think of professions where the vertical Helicopter route is the default approach? Professions that, when faced with a problem to be solved, immediately create three or four options in their mind. And then carefully proceed towards selecting the best answer over time. Can you think of some? Let me mention architects, designers, advertising agencies, sales people, entrepreneurs, etc. These professions share a belief system whereby the proper way to solve any problem is to quickly suggest a range of possible options, and then slowly progress towards the answer preferred by all the parties involved.

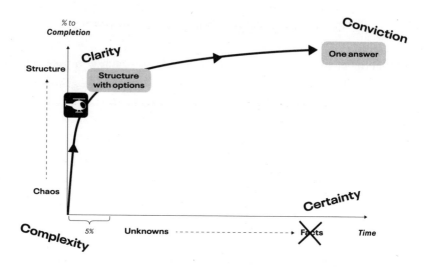

Helicopter
of Creative Discovery

For example, imagine that you ask an architect to come up with a design for a building. The answer at the end of the project is the building's design, fully approved. At the beginning of the project, the architect quickly comes up with a number of alternative designs that they run past their client. What structure do architects use to arrive at these multiple options? Various families of theories, or schools of architecture. Frank Gehry is all about angular shapes, Zaha Hadid is more fluid, the British School of Design brings boxy shapes, Le Corbusier concrete, etc. Architects have their own theories as to what constitutes an acceptable outcome, and they can very quickly create three or four options for any client.

Likewise, if you ask an agency to come up with an advertising campaign, and you give them a month, usually they'll only take a few days to generate many alternatives. They then reveal these to their client and gradually amend them over time to reach an answer that meets with the client's approval. Entrepreneurs are also great practitioners of the Helicopter ride. Quickly imagining a few options for a new business venture, in a flash of brilliance. Then twisting and turning over time, to iron out the glitches of the first version(s). Their final answer will often be more a matter of personal taste than of fact-based evidence.

So there are professions for whom the horizontal Submarine of Analytical Research is a bit bizarre, and the vertical Helicopter of Creative Discovery is a very natural approach to adopt. And vice versa, as we saw earlier.

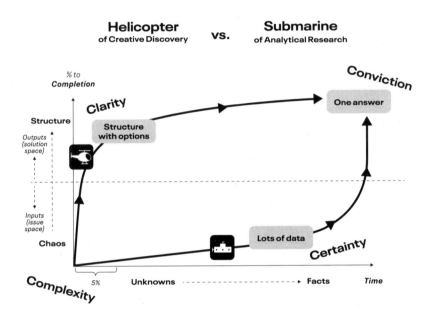

A lot of people who practise strategy and strategic thinking are very comfortable with numbers. They've often also been trained in the Submarine route in academic settings, and they use it by default. Not because they can't do the Helicopter, but because they don't know that this alternative is available and / or don't know how to use it. Conversely, a lot of people with backgrounds in the humanities, design or creative industries often find the vertical approach of quickly getting to multiple options quite straightforward.

Whatever your own background, the big benefit of the Helicopter route as a problem-solving approach is clarity. You achieve clarity quickly by discovering a range of options in no time. The corner of the map we shoot for with this approach, the top left corner on our map, rightfully deserves to be labelled the Clarity corner. It's the time and place in your project where you start envisaging what possible answers might look like.

The Helicopter of Creative Discovery is the path that problem-solving activities follow when quickly generating many creative options, without much data, to rapidly reach clarity for all stakeholders.

Those of you familiar with the work of economics Nobel Prize winner Daniel Kahneman will recognize something familiar here. Kahneman's weighty tome *Thinking, Fast and Slow* can be overlaid very neatly on our map. *Thinking Fast* is the vertical Helicopter route, quickly generating several options, and *Thinking Slow* is the horizontal Submarine route, carefully considering all the evidence before reaching a conclusion.

We've discussed before the pros and cons of the Submarine route. Let's do the same here for the Helicopter route. In the Helicopter approach you invest 5 per cent of the time allocated to you to get to the Clarity corner, build some structure and identify a few creative options. As a result of which, you'll get structure, options, clarity and four amazing additional benefits.

The first benefit is that you can choose to run these options by your stakeholder (client, boss, etc.) and they, in turn, can help you by passing judgement on these early options. 'I quite like option A, option B maybe, I'm not sure about option C.' And they can also mention other options, D or E, that you might have missed.

In the creative Helicopter route, by going up vertically you can quickly discover multiple options that look like outputs. It's not 100 per cent complete yet, but you get a range of possible creative solutions that can be discussed, assessed and added to. Comparatively, in the horizontal Submarine route you spend a huge amount of time in the input space, and you only come out with some solutions at the back end. It's a bit late for people to help you if you get it wrong.

The second benefit of the Helicopter route is that, once you have quick clarity on your options, you then have a huge amount of time to choose your preferred answer. You can work at a slightly more measured pace because you have plenty of time left on the project, as opposed to the Submarine route where people typically take a long time to gather the data at the beginning and are left with very little time to construct their answer at the end.

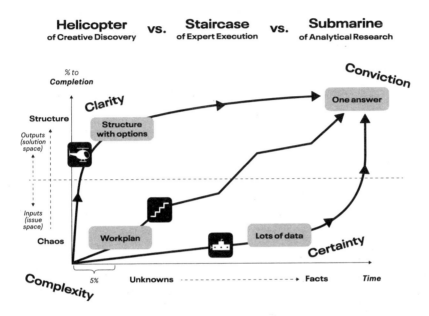

The third benefit is that you now have a much clearer sense of what you need to do to pick your favourite answers among your various early options. For example, an ad agency might redesign its mock-ups, run various drafts past stakeholders, float final versions past focus groups, etc. An entrepreneur, once she has identified a number of possible ventures, can talk to friends, sleep on it, write one-page business plans, etc. The long horizontal stretch of work from the Clarity corner to the Conviction corner involves the gentle polishing of a draft hypothesis, with often an element of personal taste and subjectivity at the heart of the chosen answer.

The fourth benefit is rather more subtle. As soon as you present a number of options and some structure to your stakeholders, they too can relax. They feel a bit more confident in your ability to solve the problem in due course. They've seen that you have some structure behind your early work.

The real benefit for them, and for you, is that they now have plenty of time to mull things over. They can get comfortable. They can discuss with their peers. They can kick the options around in their heads. Which means that when you come back, at the end, and recommend a given option X, they may not be surprised because they might have arrived at that same conclusion on their own. That makes it a lot easier to get agreement on the answer you recommend.

So, to sum up, the Helicopter of Creative Discovery is an effective way to structure your unknowns in order to arrive quickly at some options, with four great benefits:

> clarity for your stakeholders (which gives them the opportunity for input)
> clarity for yourself (which helps you work out how to pick your final answer)
> time for yourself (which means you can work at a slightly more relaxed pace until the end of the project), and
> time for your stakeholders (which allows them time to mull things over on their own).

That vertical approach is about powerful and quick thinking. The Helicopter route forces you to think creatively, using your head and your heart very early on. Thinking fast, in the words of Nobel Prize winner Daniel Kahneman. There are many benefits to the Helicopter route, and also two gigantic drawbacks.

The first drawback is the blinding blunder of brilliance. Very early in the process, one of the options can appear much shinier than all the others generated to date – whether the idea itself is indeed brilliant, or the most senior person in the room finds it so. The HiPPO curse (Highest Paid Person's Opinion) can strike early in the Helicopter approach, and the time throughout the rest of the project is then spent perfecting and polishing the chosen answer to match the HiPPO's loudly stated early preference. The other options are not taken seriously for long enough to disprove otherwise. Thinking *too* Fast.

The second drawback appears later in the project. Daniel Kahneman, in his book *Thinking, Fast and Slow*, might probably label this drawback *the wrong kind* of thinking slow, and he could also call it human nature. In business, a decision is taken more often than not by a group of people who have to report to another group of people. Imagine that your team has been careful to generate three or four equally likely – and equally liked – options early in the project (thereby avoiding the HiPPO drawback above), and multiple discussions over time have resulted in a commonly agreed, preferred solution at the end. It can be a solution that is fully backed by this group, but is likely to be very subjective, appealing to that specific group of people. What if stakeholders up the chain insist on the reassurance of data, at the end of the project? What are you to do then? In business, at every step in the decision chain, a recommended solution has to be backed up by data. Objective data travels up the chain much better than anything else. Particularly much better than the highly subjective taste preferences that the Helicopter route typically relies upon.

So, the Helicopter of Creative Discovery offers great benefits (time + clarity + creativity) and some drawbacks (HiPPO curse + data-light). Is there a better way to solve complex problems? Of course. That's where the Rollercoaster comes in.

The Rollercoaster of Strategic Thinking

The Rollercoaster of Strategic Thinking is the best approach to take **when you're faced with** the following constraints on a problem or project:

> - **no clear answer** at the beginning (so the Staircase won't work)
> - **very little data** available throughout (so the Submarine won't work), and
> - **stakeholders insist on data** at the end (so the Helicopter alone is not enough).

You can see the dilemma here. You know that there's not going to be a huge amount of data (and/or that it's going to be unreliable), but your stakeholders expect you to ground your recommendation in some Certainty. They've also told you that they'd quite like to see a number of early options, with some structure, in order to reach Clarity quickly and gain confidence in your work.

How do you reconcile all these constraints and expectations to achieve Conviction at the end? How do you set out from Complexity, thread your way through Clarity and Certainty, and arrive at Conviction?

The Rollercoaster of Strategic Thinking combines the Helicopter of Creative Discovery, at the beginning of the project, and the Submarine of Analytical Research, at the back end of the project.

The Rollercoaster of Strategic Thinking starts exactly like the Helicopter route. You go vertical early, structuring the chaos and quickly identifying a number of creative options, to get to Clarity.

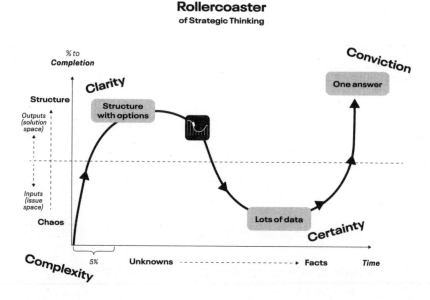

Rollercoaster
of Strategic Thinking

Once at Clarity, however, instead of taking your time to gently fine-tune your options (the way you would in the Helicopter approach), you now proactively smash them with all the data you can get – however limited the dataset available to you. This back-end stretch of analytical validation will eliminate lots of options that looked like perfectly valid answers in theory. It will make you feel that you're moving away from completion and back down to chaos. Once the fog of analysis clears, however, you will discover your best surviving answer. You can then start working on presenting this answer with Conviction, thanks to the Certainty afforded to you by the data you've manipulated.

In a nutshell: Strategic = Creative + Analytical.

Please note, in the opposite order from the order which is usually assumed. To be strategic, first be creative, then be analytical. Since strategic thinking deals with the future, you will have very little quality data available to you, and starting with analysis would be a mistake. Let's talk about professions that rely on the Rollercoaster approach by default.

We'll start with doctors. If you visit a doctor because you feel unwell, they'll quickly generate in their mind a number of options regarding the possible root causes of your illness. What structure do they use? Their knowledge of human biology, and of human health in general. Once they have Clarity, they send for tests, i.e. expose their ideas to data, and see many of these proven wrong. Hopefully, one of the tests will offer Certainty, and they'll be able to recommend a course of treatment.

Another profession? Scientists. They operate at the boundary of knowledge, discovering things that are not yet known. They typically posit a few hypotheses (aka options) on some unknown aspect of the world, and then dive into the data to test them. They fail often. Every so often they achieve a breakthrough and try to convince their peers that a new discovery has been made.

Strategists of all shapes and sizes naturally rely on the Rollercoaster too. Going up quickly by creating a few ideas for the future of their team, clients or company. Then diving into the data to eliminate the weak options. And finally constructing a great case to convince stakeholders of their recommended solution.

The Rollercoaster of Strategic Thinking always contains three distinct sections.

> - How to **Generate Great Ideas Quickly** ('Up')
> - How to **Eliminate Options in No Time** ('Down')
> - How to **Get the Best Solution Approved** ('Push')

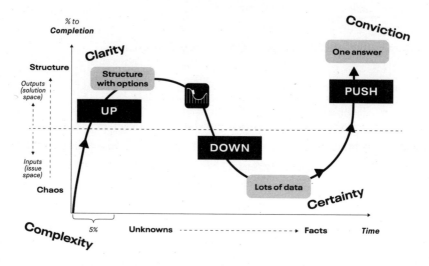

These three sections of the Rollercoaster naturally constitute the three central parts of this book. Let's introduce them briefly, in turn.

HOW TO GENERATE GREAT IDEAS QUICKLY ('UP')

This might feel quite familiar already. It is the vertical start to the Helicopter route. Create a structure and come up with a number of options early on, to reach Clarity. There are many ways to quickly get to the Clarity corner in a business context, and in the 'Up' part of this book I'll show you how to:

> craft **logic trees** that connect words with lines, to create some structure around any unfamiliar problem
> borrow from **business theories** and virtually call upon some of the best business brains in the world, to generate multiple smart options quickly, and
> use some counter-intuitive **thinking techniques** to broaden your understanding of the problem at hand, and discover highly creative options.

Remember, going vertical to Clarity early and sharing initial options gives your stakeholders time to mull things over. This means that the data you provide to support your answer when flying the Helicopter of Creative Discovery does not need to be entirely comprehensive – because your stakeholders will bring their own thinking to the equation, including their own data and taste preferences.

HOW TO ELIMINATE OPTIONS IN NO TIME ('DOWN')

If you want your strategic recommendation to be taken seriously in a business context, you need to put your options through as many validation steps as possible. We'll go through three big techniques to do exactly that in the third part of this book. When crash-testing your early options in 'Down', you will discover how to:

> employ various **qualitative techniques** to pit all your ideas against one another, and have the ideas themselves create their own ranking
> apply some of the many **quantitative techniques** available to offer a more numerically derived validation of your options to date, and
> construct **real-life tests**, whenever possible, to demonstrate in practice the viability or otherwise of each of your remaining options.

Each of the 'Down' techniques listed above is a way to offer proof of likely future success. All three techniques are quite different from the approach to data one would typically encounter in a Submarine of Analytical Research. In the Submarine approach, you gather a huge amount of data first (just in case), analyse it in dozens of ways, and then deduce a likely solution. In the Rollercoaster approach instead, you focus first on generating many ideas (the 'Up' phase), and then expose these to data (the 'Down' phase) to eliminate the weak ones.

Jeff Bezos at Amazon lists 14 key principles that his senior managers must live by. Two of these principles are 'Think Big' and 'Dive Deep'. It is relatively easy to spot how these correlate well with our notions of 'Up' and 'Down' respectively. The more strategic the issue you face, the less data there will be. Which is why you should keep your powder dry, and use whatever data there is to validate or kill ideas, not to generate them. An additional benefit to this approach is that the dataset you need to test an idea is much smaller than the dataset you need to generate an idea.

By way of example, imagine you've just had an idea for a new process or product at work. It is really easy to type this idea into Google, and the search results will tell you right away whether this idea already exists in the world. Two or three data points on the results page will help reveal whether someone else is already doing what you envisaged doing, or not. One minute and done. Imagine, by comparison, the hours of analytical research that would be required to come up with the idea itself via random searches on Google.

So 'Down' is about diving from a great height into the world of data to identify the likelihood that an idea you've already had will be successful or not. Not uncommonly, data will prove sparse, unreliable and contradictory. Unsurprisingly, you might feel at that moment that you're further away from Completion than at any point since the start of the project. Do not despair. We'll see in the 'Down' part of the book how to turn this into Certainty.

As a final comment, it is also common on some projects to experience a proper rollercoaster ride, with more than one 'Up' swing to Clarity, and more than one 'Down' dive into the world of data. Eventually, you will reach Certainty, knowing that you have at hand as robust a proof as you'll ever get, and the next step will be to convince your stakeholder.

HOW TO GET THE BEST SOLUTION APPROVED ('PUSH')

The final ascent from Certainty corner to Conviction corner requires its own set of techniques. We'll cover them in the fourth part of this book. To get your recommendation approved, in 'Push' we'll show you how to:

> harness **impactful words** to adapt your communication to the demonstrated individual preference of each stakeholder
> collate some **simple numbers** (as no idea ever gets approved

without overcoming some sort of financial hurdle), and
> craft a **compelling story** to grab your stakeholders' attention for the key aspects of your recommendation that they need to understand.

This combination of words, numbers and story will feel familiar to you. It's the combination that everyone uses to convince stakeholders at the end of any project, whatever route one has taken to get to the conclusion. An expert will offer words, numbers and story – as will a researcher, and often a creative too.

The slight difference when presenting conclusions at the end of a Rollercoaster of Strategic Thinking is the comparatively thin layer of data. When there isn't much data to share, you have to be more efficient with your numbers, more powerful with your words – and more compelling with your story!

IN SUMMARY

There are four ways to solve complex problems: Expert, Analytical, Creative, Strategic. Each of these works particularly well for certain types of problems – or certain professions. Most people use one approach for all the problems they face, instead of applying the right approach to each category of problems. We've now seen the four Routes to Completion (Staircase, Helicopter, Submarine and Rollercoaster) and introduced the three sections of the Rollercoaster of Strategic Thinking (Up–Down–Push). Let's briefly summarize before moving on.

The Staircase of Expert Execution is the right approach to take when someone (you or a third party) can credibly put their hand up and say, 'I've done it before, I know the way, follow me.' Creating a workplan very early in the process, or even before the start, is a great way for the experts to prove that the problem is not complex for them, and to convince stakeholders of the validity of their method and their answer. The Staircase approach, however, is neither good nor credible at tackling brand-new problems.

The Submarine of Analytical Research is great when there's lots of reliable data available – lying around, or to be discovered. Typically in the present or in the past. Carefully find the data, absorb it, analyse it and then deduce the answer. An inquiry, a review, an investigation, etc. All these words point to problems that have already happened. These are the types of problems for which the horizontal path is built, and analytical research is likely to yield great results. The Submarine struggles, however, as soon as the issue to be tackled is in the future.

Map of 4 Problem-Solving Routes

The Helicopter of Creative Discovery is brilliant at tackling the future. The future can't be analysed, it can only be created. Generating many creative options with limited data is what many people naturally do when they envisage future holidays or entrepreneurial ventures. This takes no time. The vertical way is exciting, light and free. The rest of the time is dedicated to slowly maturing the options, through discussion and reflection, until reaching an answer that feels right. The Helicopter approach, however, is too reliant on subjective matters of personal taste to be entirely convincing in a business context.

The Rollercoaster of Strategic Thinking is obviously the right approach to take when tackling a strategic issue at work. **A truly strategic issue manifests the following characteristics**:

> the problem is **big**
> it lies in the **future**
> it's **never been done** before
> there will likely be **very little data**
> the best answer is **not just a matter of taste**, and
> it will **require proof** to convince many stakeholders.

The Up–Down–Push rhythm of the Rollercoaster is perfectly suited to solving strategic problems. In most jobs, strategic issues are not that frequent. Which is why the majority of people spend their time solving problems with the Expert, Analytical or Creative routes for most of their career. The more senior you want to get, however, and the more successful you want to become, the more you need to be strategic. That's what being in charge really means. You've got to learn to ride the Rollercoaster of Strategic Thinking!

PART TWO

HOW TO GENERATE GREAT IDEAS QUICKLY ('UP')

There are many ways to quickly get to the Clarity corner in a business context, and we mentioned in **How to Solve Complex Problems** ('Think'), that you could:

> - craft **logic trees**, that connect words with lines, to create some structure around any unfamiliar problem
> - borrow from **business theories** and virtually call upon some of the best business brains in the world, to generate multiple smart options quickly, and
> - use some counter-intuitive **thinking techniques** to broaden your understanding of the problem at hand, and discover highly creative options.

In this part, **How to Generate Great Ideas Quickly** ('Up'), we'll examine one technique from each family:

> - a **logic tree:** the **Pyramid Principle**
> - a **business theory:** the **Happy Line**, and
> - a **thinking technique:** the **Mutation Game**.

Let's take a step back for a second. What is the most common way for a group of between four and 20 people to come up with lots of ideas in under an hour? Brainstorming. The unstructured and dynamic interplay of preconceived notions, reheated ideas, flashes of brilliance and HiPPO syndrome (Highest Paid Person's Opinion). Nothing wrong with a good brainstorm. As long as you're prepared to acknowledge the three big limitations of brainstorming: you can never be sure that you've covered the whole spectrum of ideas; you can't always explain how ideas came about; and you can't explain why they will be any good. The three techniques for 'Up' that we will explore in this part force the participants to be much more structured, resulting in a comprehensive universe of ideas and better trackability for each idea. Each technique revolves around a specific question.

The Pyramid Principle is wonderful for convergent thinking (when you're pretty sure you're looking at the right outcome, but you don't have a path yet) and gives you Clarity through repeatedly asking, 'What would need to be true to achieve the success we seek?' The Mutation Game is better at divergent thinking (when you're sure of the starting point but less clear on your destination) and gives you lots of ideas by asking, 'What more successful versions of our business lie on the edge of our consciousness?' The Happy Line is a halfway house, leading you to both Clarity and some ideas by asking, 'How well are we currently meeting our customers' needs and expectations?'

Any good session of 'Up' thinking probably combines any two of these three techniques over a few hours – one after the other, or in parallel in smaller groups.

2

PYRAMID PRINCIPLE

Using the Pyramid Principle at the beginning of projects

The Pyramid Principle is a brilliant technique that can be used to structure one's thinking at two different stages in the life of a project or problem-solving activity. It can be used at the end of the project, for Conviction, to structure a presentation to convince an audience of the validity of your recommendations – after you have achieved the answer. We will cover this later in the book. Let's start by looking at how the Pyramid Principle can also be used early in a project, for Clarity, to discover the underlying structure of a qualitative issue and quickly identify a convergent path to success. Before you have the answer.

Rollercoaster
of Strategic Thinking

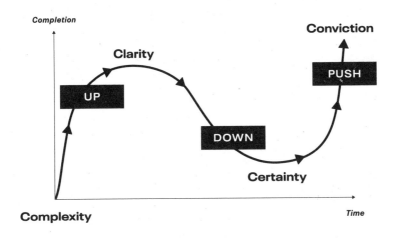

First, what is a qualitative issue? In a business or personal context, qualitative issues are questions like: 'Should we be doing X?', 'How can we be more successful at Y?', 'How much support should we give Z?', etc. These questions are the most common in business, and are typically answered by words rather than numbers. (Or at least you can look for a words-based answer rather than a numbers-based one.) The words-based answers to the three questions might be 'Yes, let's do X', or 'No, let's not do X', or 'Invest a lot more in Y', or 'Let's cancel Z'.

You may already be aware that a lot of anxiety at work comes from the inability to easily answer some questions that start with the word 'how'. When you already know the answer, 'how' questions are wonderful, and they nicely reinforce your expert status. When you don't know the answer, however, 'how' questions are very stressful, with expectations from your stakeholders (boss, direct reports, customers, etc.) often working to tight deadlines. The Pyramid Principle is a wonderful way to generate great ideas quickly when you don't know the answer to the question 'How?', or 'Should we?'

SEVEN TIPS ON USING THE PYRAMID PRINCIPLE AT THE BEGINNING OF PROJECTS

Here are my seven tips for using the Pyramid Principle early in the life of a project.

1. Write at the top of your work surface the **most desirable outcome**, or the most difficult one to achieve.
2. Populate and structure a pyramid of Post-its below, with the answers to two simple questions:

   - going down: 'What would **need to be true** for this to be true?'
   - going back up: 'Can we think of a scenario where the three Post-its below are true, and yet the one **above is not automatically true**?'

3. Try and follow a **MECE** logic in the pyramid.
4. Gradually replace buzzwords with **full sentences** in the building blocks.

5. Write the sentences as **positive statements** rather than negative ones or questions.

6. Re-order the building blocks for most critical storytelling.

7. Continue to the **next level down**.

Each tip will become second nature to you over time. In the meantime, let's go into further depth on each.

1. Write the most desirable outcome

My first tip is to write at the top (of a blank page or a flipchart) the most desirable outcome, or the most difficult one to achieve. Instead of 'How do we do X?' you write 'We are doing X very successfully', or 'We should be doing Y', or 'We do Z successfully by next year', etc. We're going to use as an example a qualitative issue from the realm of personal life, one that many of you will be familiar with.

Imagine that you are getting married in six months' time, and your romantic partner is really nervous. One night, he or she wakes up in a sweat in the middle of the night, asking you, 'Is our wedding going to be a great success?' or, 'How are we going to make our wedding a great wedding?' You can try to reassure him or her, and reply, 'Don't worry, it'll be fine.' You would be making a leap of faith, though, between now and an outcome that's six months away. Your strong and resolute answer is not very credible, since you don't have any real data on the future, nor any expertise on the issue. Let's pretend instead that you're both strategic thinkers, and that you decide to apply the Pyramid Principle, there and then, to achieve Clarity on your issue.

Following my tip, the first thing you do is write on a big Post-it on a wall or window: 'Our wedding is a great success.' Move the conversation from 'how to achieve X' to 'X has been achieved successfully'. Already the tension goes away a little bit. You can visualize and feel your wedding becoming a great success.

2. Populate and structure

Under this top Post-it, you then ask yourself two questions to populate the next level down.

The first question is: 'What would need to be true for this to be true?' Typically, you look to write three Post-its at the next level down.

You might write here if 'both romantic partners are there and happy'. And if 'all the guests are there and happy'. And if 'the logistics and the weather are perfect'. Then 'our wedding is a great success'. You've started to populate your pyramid one level down. We call this a pyramid, as it will start to look like one when you have two or three more levels in your structure.

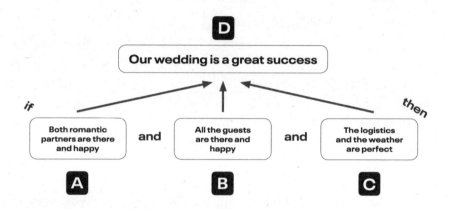

The second question you then use, to tighten your first draft, is: 'Can we think of a scenario under which all three A, B and C conditions below are true, and yet the D outcome on the line above is not automatically true?' So can we think of a scenario here under which 'both romantic partners are there and happy', 'all the guests are there and happy', 'the logistics and the weather are perfect', and yet the wedding is not automatically a great success? Some people might say if 'the photographer doesn't show up', or if 'the celebrant is not there', or if 'we run out of drinks', or if 'the venue gets too hot', etc.

What do you do now? You've effectively identified tougher conditions for success, so you just update the corresponding Post-its with those tougher conditions. You replace 'both romantic partners are there and happy' with 'both romantic partners are there and happy, and all the additional key people for the ceremony (celebrant, photographer, best man, bridesmaids, etc.) are there, prepared and ready'. The second condition could be rewritten as 'all the guests are there and happy, with perfect quantity and quality of drinks, food and music, etc.' You can see that we've made the new versions of conditions A and B tougher to achieve. At the same time, if those new, tougher conditions are met, then the outcome in the line above is closer to being automatically true.

Every time you think of a new objection, you add it to the corresponding Post-it. You make each condition harder, and harder, and harder to achieve. You'll then reach a point when, looking at the three Post-its in a row in the pyramid, you won't be able to think of any additional circumstances under which, if these three are true, the outcome in the Post-it above is not automatically true.

This is the alchemy of the Pyramid Principle. It helps you turn objections into structure, early on in a project. Objections are an abundant base metal of life (i.e. everyone is happy to tell you what might go wrong with your project). The Pyramid Principle at the point of Clarity helps you quickly turn this base metal into pure gold (i.e. a clear, logical and rigorous structure for the problem you need to tackle, including conditions for success).

3. Follow a MECE logic

My third tip helps you structure each level in your pyramid. ME stands for Mutually Exclusive, and CE for Completely Exhaustive. Completely Exhaustive means the sum total of the three Post-its below covers all the content contained in the one above. That is really important. You don't want to lose some aspects of the issue as you go from one level to the next one down. Mutually Exclusive is a bit less critical. It simply means you don't count something twice. Arguably, it is better to err on the side of caution than to fail. Better to count something twice than to forget it altogether. In our wedding planning example, you're better off counting the father of the bride both in the 'key people in the ceremony' and in the 'guests' Post-its, rather than forgetting him altogether.

4. Gradually replace buzzwords by full sentences

When starting a pyramid, you might want to reach for buzzwords ('guests', 'logistics', etc.). Buzzwords help you go fast, and populate several levels in your pyramid in one go. My fourth tip is to think of these as a first draft, and gradually start replacing the buzzwords by full sentences. In our example, we get two benefits when we replace the buzzword 'guests' by the sentence 'all the guests are there and happy'.

The first benefit is that it helps the wedding organizers have a slightly broader appreciation of any issue, like 'guests' in our example. One person might say, 'How about if some of the guests are not there?' And someone else might well say, 'What if some of the guests are unhappy?' You put in the Post-it a sentence that reads, 'All the guests are there and happy.' So you reconcile both contributions in one go.

The second benefit you get with that longer sentence is that it's a lot easier to trickle down to the next level. Because once you've written 'all the guests are there and happy', you can then ask what needs to be true for that to be true? Well, if 'all the guests are there', and if 'all the guests are happy now', and if 'all the guests have great memories', then 'all the guests are there and happy'. Using a longer sentence in the above Post-it makes it easier to populate the three Post-its below.

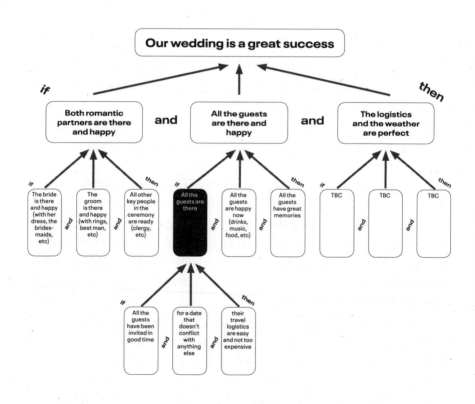

Let's go one step further and look at 'all the guests are there'. What needs to be true for that to be true? Well, if 'all the guests have been invited in good time', 'for a date that doesn't conflict with anything else' (like another friend's wedding), and 'the logistics are easy and not too expensive', then 'all the guests are there'.

Once you're in the habit, you just need to use these two sentences. First: 'What needs to be true for this level to be true?' This helps you create a first draft of the three Post-its below. Then ask yourself: 'Can I think of a scenario under which these three are true, and yet the one above is not true?' If you can think of one, then add the words in the relevant Post-it to make the conditions a bit tougher, and the logical structure a bit tighter. If you can't think of one, then it's time to go one level down.

Quite often, you might have the three Post-its you like, and another member of the team suggests there is a fourth possible one. In our example above, what if someone is sick the night before? The temptation is strong to dedicate a fourth Post-it to 'no unforeseen circumstances', and add it to the pyramid. I recommend, however, that you don't do this. By all means, do write down the fourth Post-it, but then ask yourselves, 'How do these four into three go?' Find a way to re-cut the split between the current four Post-its so that you still end up with only three. In our example, we can fit the new 'unforeseen circumstances' addition as one of three components to the next level down under 'not conflicting with anything else'.

5. Use positive statements

My fifth tip is to always write sentences as positive expressions rather than negative ones, or posing questions. Write 'all the guests are there', rather than 'will all the guests be there?' or 'no guest will be missing'. Questions and negative expressions create anxieties that we could do without, early on in a project. If you write 'all the guests are there', and then ask yourself what would need to be true for that to be true, it's more positive and you'll progress the logic further. If you write instead 'will all the guests be there?' you immediately fuel your anxieties about an event that is six months away and for which you have no data. It's better to focus on the structure.

6. Re-order the building blocks

At this early stage in your thinking, the pyramid is a way to put together a batch of sufficient conditions. We use the expression 'what would need to be true' to create a level of urgency in your quest for possible difficulties. Once these difficulties are identified, however, it is easy to spot that not all of them – if any at all – are equally critical or necessary to achieving the desired outcome.

In our wedding example, 'the weather is fantastic' is clearly not as critical to the success of the wedding as 'both romantic partners are there and happy'. A story is told more effectively when, in any group of conditions, the most necessary one is put on the left, and the least necessary one on the right.

7. Continue to the next level down

This is my seventh and final tip. When you have a go at a structure down to three Post-its, then nine, then 27, etc., you will likely notice that your pyramid is a bit skewed, with a lot more elements on one side than on the other. Try to populate the corner that's not as populated. Alternatively, revisit your current structure and rebalance the weight, so you have something that's a bit more evenly distributed. I call it 'smoothing the pyramid'. It means your structure will sort of work to start with, and then, gradually, as you move Post-its around, you slightly restructure the building blocks. Over time you arrive at something where the logic flows really well. You've taken a really big qualitative question (for example, 'Is our wedding going to be a great success?') and turned it into a clarifying structure that is quite detailed. You've turned your big worrying problem into three, nine, 27, 81, etc. much smaller items. And the list of these smaller items is effectively your workplan. All the stuff you need to get done to achieve your big desired outcome.

In the wedding planning example, newlyweds reinvent the pyramid of a successful wedding all the time. Some do it well, others less so. Wedding planners have that pyramid in their back pocket, and they can apply that same structure to every wedding they work on, without having to reconstruct it.

In summary

Whatever your own line of work, as a strategic thinker you know that issues are going to come at you that you haven't seen before. So you can't really fall back on a pre-existing road map for event planning. Instead, you have to construct one. A new road map, from scratch, for every single qualitative issue you have to tackle. You have to generate dozens of ideas quickly, to help you reach your outcome.

Using my seven tips, it's not too hard to take any qualitative question or problem and turn it into a very comprehensive workplan, in no time. Just remember to use the Pyramid Principle at the beginning of projects.

Strategic Pyramid examples

We are now going to see two illustrations of Strategic Pyramids in practice, and I would invite you to treat these as both examples and exercises. Have a go at both on your own for a few minutes, before reading my suggested solutions.

The first illustration is a project I did for Harley-Davidson, a few years ago. They were thinking of building their branded apparel and clothes presence in Europe in a big way. The question was really: 'Should they go ahead with that, or not?' It's a qualitative question, with a relatively binary answer, yes or no.

What I suggest to you is to put a big Post-it at the top of your page where you write: 'Harley-Davidson should enter the apparel market in Europe in a big way.' Remember from my tips about using the pyramid at the point of Clarity, that we put at the top the most contentious, most desirable outcome. Go two levels down next. Break the top Post-it into three, and then break each one of these into three as well, resulting at the bottom in nine components that would need to be true for Harley-Davidson to conclude that, 'Yes we should enter the apparel market in Europe in a big way.'

I keep using the word 'Post-its', and you're familiar with it by now. If you write with pencil on a page, you tend to get wedded to the first structure you come up with, whereas with Post-its you can chop and change and alter the priority of some of the ideas you have, bundle things in a more intelligent way quickly, etc. Why don't you take a minute now, and have a go at a pyramid for the Harley-Davidson example? I'll share with you a possible answer shortly, but you'll take this on board all the better if you've had a go at it yourself first!

Our second example is a project for the Emir of Dubai. Dubai has a media city, a place where lots of media companies are located near one another, in the same corner of Dubai. One of the Emirate's big questions was whether they should turn that small media city into a giant global media hub, where all the big media companies in the world have an office of some sort?

What you put at the top of your pyramid here is: 'Dubai is a global media hub within 10 years.' The question we're trying to address is a strategic one (should Dubai do it), not an operational one (how to do it). So, what would need to be true for Dubai to decide intelligently to go ahead with this initiative? This is a fascinating case, and I'll give you a much more detailed answer because I've done this exercise very regularly. It's really well worth your while taking a good 30 minutes to break this issue down into three, nine and 27 Post-its.

Let's now have a look at possible solutions.

HARLEY-DAVIDSON

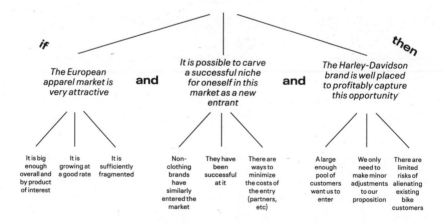

'Harley-Davidson should enter the apparel market in Europe in a big way'

if ... *then*

The European apparel market is very attractive

and

It is possible to carve a successful niche for oneself in this market as a new entrant

and

The Harley-Davidson brand is well placed to profitably capture this opportunity

It is big enough overall and by product of interest — It is growing at a good rate — It is sufficiently fragmented

Non-clothing brands have similarly entered the market — They have been successful at it — There are ways to minimize the costs of the entry (partners, etc)

A large enough pool of customers want us to enter — We only need to make minor adjustments to our proposition — There are limited risks of alienating existing bike customers

There are three branches for the challenge at hand: 'The European apparel market is very attractive', 'It is possible to carve a successful niche for oneself in this market as a new entrant' and 'The Harley-Davidson brand is well placed to profitably capture this opportunity'. We don't know yet, at the beginning of the project, what the actual answer will turn out to be. But if all three statements prove true after we've done the research, then it will be a no-brainer that Harley-Davidson should enter the European apparel market in a big way.

EMIR OF DUBAI

Now let's take a look at the Dubai exercise. It's a lot harder than the other. You'll find below five illustrations to do it justice: one for the first row of three Post-its; one each for the A, B and C blocks; then one for the overall pyramid, down to 27 Post-its.

I recommend you take the time to do this exercise properly on your own. A possible solution awaits you below. Spend 30 minutes creating your own pyramid first. Compare and contrast in due course. It will be so much more enlightening!

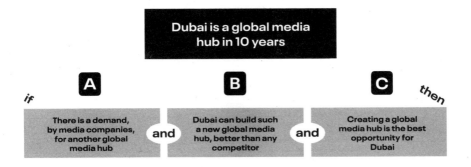

A

if → **There is a demand, by media companies, for another global media hub** ← *then*

Existing global media hubs are not meeting the needs of media companies	**and**	Hubs continue to be the favourite form of location for media companies	**and**	Media companies are willing and able to move to new locations
Media companies have evolving needs, triggered by their continuous journey towards digital fulfilment	Existing media hubs are offering sub-optimal conditions (expensive, cramped, old technology, etc)	Existing media hubs don't feel drastically compelled to evolve	A hub approach continues to offer benefits to companies (shared staffing, shared facilities, serendipity, co-creation, etc)	The benefits of de-centralized locations (cheaper facilities, cheaper staff, etc) do not outweigh the negatives	Hubbing in culturally active global cities continues to be the preferred life choice of media employees	The demand for media by consumers continues to grow, and becomes more global in its consumption	Media as a sector continues to be dominated by a few large organizations who can influence the location of an ecosystem	These large media companies have found a way to stay profitable in the digital age, and can afford to relocate

B

if → **Dubai can build such a new global media hub, better than any competitor** ← *then*

Dubai can assemble the best package of hard infrastructure for media companies	**and**	Dubai can assemble the best package of soft infrastructure for media companies	**and**	Dubai can assemble the best package for employees of media companies
Dubai has all the funds and political will needed to invest in building the infrastructure to world-class level	Dubai offers the best media-specific infrastructure (studios, ultra high-speed internet access, publishing, etc)	Dubai offers the best general business infrastructure (airports, buildings, transport, etc)	Dubai offers the very best business-friendly environment (low taxes, light regulations, rule of law, etc)	Dubai offers an abundant supply of qualified talent (management, specialists, support staff) to media companies	Dubai offers attractive incentives for media companies to relocate some or all of their operations to the new hub	Dubai offers plentiful job opportunities, and multiple professional development opportunities (universities, professional courses, etc)	Dubai is a great place for the 20- and 30-year-old employees of media companies to enjoy life the way they like it (culture, art, bars, etc)	Dubai offers a quality of life without equal for the families of the 40- and 50-year-old managers who decide on the re-location of the companies

C

if → **Creating a global media hub is the best opportunity for Dubai** ← *then*

A global media hub is in itself a very attractive investment for Dubai	**and**	A global media hub offers additional, sustainable side-benefits	**and**	No other investment option delivers for Dubai the same net benefits
A global media hub offers a positive and sizeable return on investment to the state, and to the private contractors running the hub	A global media hub offers job opportunities for Emirati nationals, the highly qualified ones and the less qualified ones	A global media hub helps reinforce the global image of Dubai as a place of comparative freedom in the Middle East	A global media hub helps foster a culture of innovation and openness, essential for the long-term future of a state without natural resources	A global media hub is the most sought after and politically acceptable option for all the locals (Emirati nationals, and global expats)	Any downside factors in creating a global media hub (cultural, political, etc) can be managed and mitigated over time	No other investment option offers the same level of positive benefits (financial, political, cultural, PR, etc)	No other investment option is as strategically aligned to Dubai's vision of becoming one of the Top 5 Global Cities	No other investment option is less risky than the comparatively simple creation of a global media hub

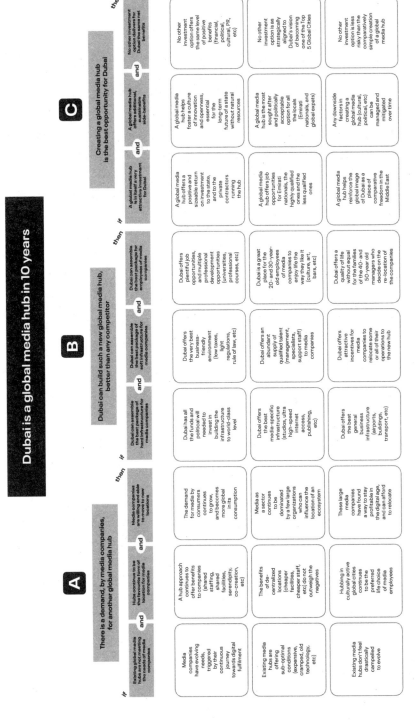

The quadruple benefits of the Pyramid Principle

The Pyramid Principle was discovered by Barbara Minto, the first female consultant at McKinsey, a few decades ago. The focus of her book *The Pyramid Principle: Logic in Thinking and Writing* is very much on how to structure a convincing presentation at the end of your project, once you've got a clear answer.

A well-crafted pyramid, generated early in a project, gives you three other, great benefits in addition to the structure for your final presentation: early calmness, a comprehensive workplan and a decision tree.

EARLY CALMNESS

The early calmness appears when you realize that a huge problem can be broken down into smaller, more manageable chunks – and which chunks exactly. For example, that a wedding can be structured into 'ceremony', 'reception' and 'other logistics', or that a global media hub in Dubai is a function of 'demand', 'supply' and 'benefits'. And that these, in turn, can be broken down into smaller sub-components.

COMPREHENSIVE WORKPLAN

The comprehensive workplan comes from the bottom part of the pyramid. All these Post-its in the bottom row (be they 27, 81, 243, etc.) are the small things that need to be undertaken for your desired outcome to come true. 'Make a list of all invitees to the wedding', 'Get their exact email address', 'Choose a font for the invitation', etc. The pyramid has delivered at one and the same time both early calmness and a comprehensive workplan, usually in under one hour.

DECISION TREE

Over time, as the results from the workplan start coming in, you'll notice that the pyramid also becomes a decision tree. Visualize the pyramid upside down, with the desired outcome now at the bottom, and the smaller Post-its all in a row at the top. In this configuration, the results of your work will trickle down into a specific version of the outcome. In the wedding example, if the music has to be provided by your nephew's teenage band, and the food is finger buffet, you will achieve a different successful wedding than if the music is provided by Beyoncé playing live, and the catering comes from some fancy chef. The upside-down pyramid is now a decision tree, helping you work out what exact version of the outcome you are likely to achieve based on the results of your workplan and your work.

CONVINCING PRESENTATION

Finally, once the data is fully in, the Pyramid Principle is indeed a great way to structure a convincing presentation. For example, to convince the Emir of Dubai to go ahead, or not, with investing in building a global media hub. I will give you specific tips on how best to use the Pyramid Principle at the end of projects, and we'll cover these in the 'Compelling Story' chapter in Part Four of this book.

Pyramid Principle exercise: How to have a great life?

The Pyramid Principle is a technique used to achieve a desirable outcome. Whatever outcome you desire. It clearly works well in a business context, to help turn all these 'how do we achieve X' questions into clear plans of actions. It also works well in a personal context. Let's use the Pyramid Principle to help you achieve a great life.

The first step is to write at the top of a page the most desirable outcome, which in this instance could be: 'My life is a great success in 10 years' time.' Then ask yourself what would need to be true for this to be true. There are clearly many ways to create the first level below the desired outcome. Here are four possible ones.

> * *If* [I'm healthy] *and* [I'm wealthy] *and* [I'm happy] *then* . . .
> * Or *if* [my life is a great success according to me] *and* [my life is a great success according to my loved ones] *and* [my life is a great success according to society] *then* . . .

> Or *if* [my life is a great success in the coming three years] *and* [my life is a great success in the next four years] *and* [my life is a great success accordingly in the following three years] *then* . . .

> Or *if* [my life has been a great success over the last 10 years] *and* [my life is a great success then] *and* [my future life is a great success from then on] *then* . . .

Whenever you pencil a draft that works for you, at any level in the pyramid, the next step is to ask yourself if you can think of a scenario where the three Post-its in this level are true, and yet the one above is not automatically true. Taking this approach three levels down, all the way to 27 Post-its, will give you great clarity, possibly a small shock of self-awareness, and a great plan of action.

We have two exercises for you to practise your Pyramid Principle skills now, and we invite you to share your solutions on www.strategic. how/pyramid:

> **Pyramid Principle exercise #1**
fill in the 27 blank Post-its in Isabelle's pyramid.

> **Pyramid Principle exercise #2**
identify an alternative way to write the top three Post-its for your life (different from the four ways listed above), and fill in the 39 blank Post-its in the Pyramid of your life.

PYRAMID PRINCIPLE EXERCISE #1:
ISABELLE'S LIFE

My life is a great success in 10 years' time

if / *then*

I'm healthy
- Sane mind
- Fit body
- Rounded soul

I'm wealthy
- Steady job
- Nice savings
- Initial assets

I'm happy
- Wonderful romance
- Close family
- Warm friends

PYRAMID PRINCIPLE EXERCISE #2:
YOUR LIFE

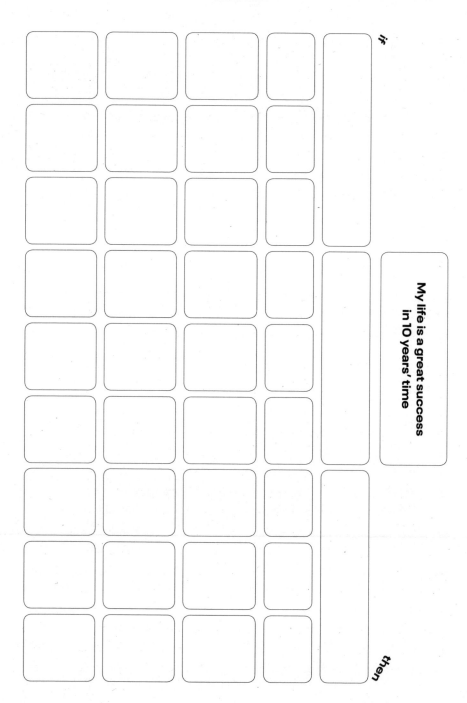

if

My life is a great success in 10 years' time

then

3.

HAPPY LINE

The Happy Line of customer satisfaction

Professor Chan Kim offers a simple and powerful take on business. He summarizes it as the fight between competitors to fulfil customers' needs and expectations: two forces, supply and demand, in a pure interplay. Since we have only two forces, we can plot these in a two-dimensional framework, with some data.

In Professor Kim's framework, we use the horizontal axis for the demand side. To populate it, we ask: 'Dear Customer, what are the key purchasing criteria that really matter to you in procuring this service or product?' We then use the vertical axis for the supply side, and we ask customers again: 'Dear Customer, how well are suppliers X, Y, Z doing on these dimensions of importance to you?'

You'll notice that, in this framework, the key articulating principle is the criteria used by customers, referred to as key purchasing criteria (KPCs). We've now created a graph with two axes, one each for the demand side and the supply side. You can plot the results of different suppliers on these dimensions. A series of black dots represents a kind of school report on supplier X, as written by customers (with the KPCs in decreasing order of importance from left to right).

If you ask customers questions about the competition, the horizontal axis will stay the same, because the criteria are generic to customers in that particular market, and then the vertical scores will be different. Different suppliers will fare very differently on the different dimensions of customer preferences. If you stop here, it's a fantastic way to describe dynamics in a market, and arguably a framework that people in market research have been using for quite a while. The real insight of Professor Kim is to come up with three more prescriptions that elevate this simple market research framework into a powerful theory of business strategy.

Happy Line Framework

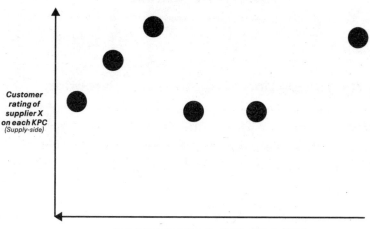

Customer ranking of Key Purchasing Criteria (KPCs)
(Demand-side)

The first prescription is that he posits the existence, in any market, of a Happy Line of customer satisfaction. In essence, a specific shape in the position of the dots that maximizes happiness for customers. He contends that customer satisfaction is not achieved when a supplier delivers 10 out of 10 on all criteria (customers know that would be unsustainable, and there would have to be a catch). Nor is customer satisfaction maximized by a supplier delivering 9 out of 10 on all criteria, or even 8 out of 10. The Happy Line of customer satisfaction is effectively a lazy L, shaped a bit like a hockey stick. In plain English, to succeed brilliantly in a market, a supplier has first to be great on the criteria that matter most to customers (i.e. the left side of the graph). As criteria matter a bit less, it's okay to be a bit less than great, up to a point where the criteria are not that important, and then it's okay to be merely good. Hence the lazy L curve for the Happy Line.

The second prescription is that to succeed in a market, you first have to find and draw the Happy Line of customer satisfaction. We'll see shortly how to do that.

The third prescription becomes interesting. Let's look at this series of black dots in the illustration below. The supplier X being mapped

The Happy Line

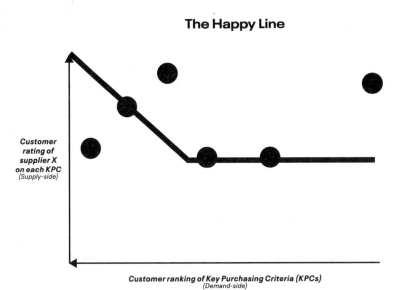

Customer rating of supplier X on each KPC
(Supply-side)

Customer ranking of Key Purchasing Criteria (KPCs)
(Demand-side)

here, whether it's you or a competitor, is not perfectly on the Happy Line. Let's pretend it's the market leader in your industry. What that suggests is that there are some opportunities for you to do better. How?

First, on the left side of the graph, on criteria that really matter to customers, we can try to come up with something that satisfies them a lot better than the current incumbent does. So let's spend a lot of time thinking about new ways to achieve a much higher rating by customers on these particular dimensions – whether it's new product, new services, new methodologies, etc.

Let's now take a look at the right side of the graph. You can see a few criteria, and one on which the current market leader is doing really well. But we actually don't need to provide that high level of satisfaction on this dimension, since the actual criteria are not that important to customers. Therefore, the vertical gap between the horizontal part of the Happy Line and the dot achieved by the market leader measures a kind of over-investment. You should not invest as much to achieve that level of performance. Take the spare cash instead, and recycle it towards the dimensions that matter more to customers, towards the left side of the graph (remember that the horizontal axis points to the left in a Happy Line framework).

Happy Line Theory

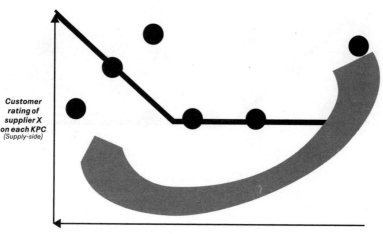

**Customer
rating of
supplier X
on each KPC**
(Supply-side)

Customer ranking of Key Purchasing Criteria (KPCs)
(Demand-side)

The first time this Happy Line was used was to help a Japanese car manufacturer that was looking to enter the luxury car market. The picture that emerged was not dissimilar to the illustration below. This suggested that the market leader, let's call it B-Merc-A (a composite of BMW, Mercedes and Audi) was doing reasonably well, because it was close enough to the Happy Line on most criteria.

As a caveat, though, the dimensions where B-Merc-A was on the line tended to be in the middle of the customer ranking of KPCs, and there was one on the very left on which customers were less enthusiastic. They weren't saying that B-Merc-A was bad, just that they were average on this important dimension. Since this was the most important criterion for customers, this clearly presented a new entrant with a great opportunity to wow customers. The second discovery was on the right of the graph. There was one criterion on which customers were saying, 'Well done, B-Merc-A, but that's not that important to me.' This presented our new entrant with the opportunity to avoid over-investing.

In real life, the most important criterion turned out to be service, and the least important one was top speed. The graph screams to us that customers want someone to launch a car with much higher service,

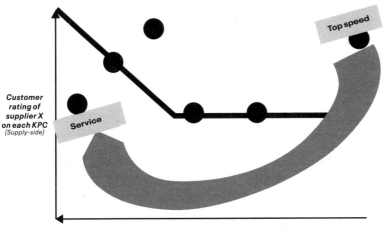

Happy Line for Luxury Car Markets
(plotting B-Merc-A for all customers)

Customer rating of supplier X on each KPC (Supply-side)

Service

Top speed

Customer ranking of Key Purchasing Criteria (KPCs)
(Demand-side)

even if it comes with a lower top speed. This would have been a mind-boggling business strategy recommendation for the petrolheads of the car industry at the time. Invest less in the engine to be able to spend more on delivering a better service? Madness!

This recommendation, however, was logically derived from the badly met needs of customers at the time, and would have been well worth exploring and testing further. The Japanese car manufacturer we mentioned earlier did just that. Great service, average top speed . . . this is how Lexus was born, created by Toyota to become the most successful new luxury car brand ever (until Tesla appeared on the scene).

A nice additional benefit that Toyota/Lexus gained from using the Happy Line is a much smoother financial ride, and far less risk at launch. Moving from the engine towards service shifts the cost base away from fixed costs (R&D + production overheads) towards variable costs (service), and from upfront to ex-post costs. Thanks to the Happy Line, Lexus would incur costs only after, and in proportion to, the success of its venture, rather than a large fixed amount upfront. Smart.

What we've seen so far about the Happy Line can be summarized in three steps:

> diagnostic
> trade-offs, and
> ideas.

First the diagnostic. You identify the KPCs. I would suggest here that you start with the market as a whole. More often than not, when you do a Happy Line for the market as a whole, you'll find that the market leader is reasonably close to the line. That's a reasonable expectation. If the market leader isn't, you find yourself with a huge opportunity. If the market leader is close to the Happy Line, as expected, you then proceed to the next level down.

You split your market into three or four segments, and you do a Happy Line for each. There will be at least one segment in which the market leader will be much further away from the Happy Line for that segment. That's your entry point. Of course, if you happen to be the dominant incumbent, then that segment is your Achilles heel and you should fix it right away.

In this first diagnostic stage you always identify the customer KPCs, construct a profile of yourself or the competitor you want to take on, and then draw the line of customer satisfaction prevailing in your market or sub-segments (more on this later).

The second step in the method is to identify the trade-offs. Focus the bulk of your efforts on the most important KPCs. The Happy Line is a phenomenal 80/20 tool. In any market there are zillions of KPCs. Typically, marketing departments love to deal with the easy KPCs, the ones towards the right of the graph. Strategists have to really look hard at the most important KPCs, find ways to improve these, and not waste too many resources on the rest. The marketing zone is usually the top right, and the strategy zone is the bottom left. As a rule, the Happy Line theory ends up taking from the fluffy marketing zone, and recycling towards the tougher strategy zone.

The third and final step is the ideas generation itself. Once you've identified the trade-offs available to you (the Post-its or dots that are below the line on the left, and the ones above the line on the right), there are actually lots of ways in which you can link them, to achieve transformation. In the case of Lexus, they chose to invest more in service than in top speed. Sometimes it may be about combining these two

KPCs in new creative ways. This third step of ideas generation is where you should spend most time. It's quite nifty in practice, and very insightful. We'll see a detailed, practical example shortly.

The Happy Line started life as a business strategy theory, and we've seen that it works beautifully to help you create a brand-new business from scratch, the way it did for Toyota with Lexus. Professor Kim has expanded greatly on this in his best-selling book *Blue Ocean Strategy: How to Create Uncontested Market Space and Make the Competition Irrelevant*.

Away from corporate strategy, the Happy Line works brilliantly in lots of other strategic contexts: to help a business unit, a department, a function, a team, or just one person do better. The Happy Line is, in effect, a strategic technique designed to help anyone do better by increasing the satisfaction of the stakeholders they serve. Don't treat people as *you* would like to be treated, treat them as *they* would like to be treated.

Let's see a couple more examples and an exercise.

Happy Line example

To see how the Happy Line works in practice, pick a brand of train company that you're familiar with and imagine you are the COO. It could be Avanti in the UK, Amtrak in the US, NSW TrainLink in Australia, or any other company you know, as long as they operate trains.

As COO of Avanti (or whatever brand you pick) you are aware that the company isn't performing as well as it should do, and you'd like to see if the Happy Line construct will help. You gather your senior team around a flipchart. With a marker you split the page in two horizontally, and draw in the top half of the page the two axes of the Happy Line. The horizontal axis is for key customer criteria (remember, the arrow points to the left). The vertical axis is for the customer ratings on each of the KPCs. From here you can follow a six-step process that will be quick and effective. To keep things simple, start with a Happy Line just for business travel.

Take some Post-its and delegate responsibility to a member of your team, Person 1, and invite them to write down 10 to 12 KPCs. As Person

1 starts writing, you invite everyone in the team to suggest ideas, shouting them or whispering them. Person 1 is in charge of writing these on Post-its, with complete freedom to accept or reject the suggestions from the rest of the team. The list of KPCs they identify here are likely to include speed, punctuality, comfort, catering, onboard facilities, etc.

Once Person 1 is done, the second person in the team takes over. The role of Person 2 is to double-check that list, and they're allowed to change maybe two of the Post-its. For example, they may believe that sandwiches or catering are not as important as price, and they select price instead.

Now that we have a final list of 10 to 12 KPCs, Person 3 ranks these KPCs in decreasing order of importance. We eliminate the least important criteria (typically anything above six to eight). Then Person 4 has a go at swapping the ranking order of a maximum of two out of the remaining six to eight KPCs. Next, Person 5 rates Avanti on the vertical dimension. What would customers say about Avanti if they were in the room? How satisfied would they be on each KPC? Finally, Person 6 is allowed to change vertically only two of the Post-its.

This is a process that takes longer to explain than to carry out in practice. You will have noticed that a specific member of the team is in absolute command of the process at any point in time. It makes things faster. Also, because each person controls only a small portion of the whole process, by the time you're finished, the Happy Line that you end up with is nobody's favourite idea. It's properly a collective achievement. Another way to put it is that nobody is particularly happy with it, and so nobody is too defensive about it. The fastest teams can arrive at that final output in under two minutes flat. It can be an extraordinarily quick process.

Once you have the dots in place, the next step is to decide where to draw the line. This actually doesn't really matter. You know that it starts on the top left, then it sort of slopes down, hits a point of inflection, and then continues horizontally all the way to the right. So the only question is, where is the point of inflection?

Rather than ask yourself where is the point, just imagine below five different possible versions of the line: versions 1, 2, 3, 4 and 5. If the

Happy Line was completely horizontal on 10 out of 10 (version 1), then we'd be terrible at everything and there'd be no point in doing the exercise. If the Happy Line of customer satisfaction went down too fast (version 5), then we'd be fantastic at everything and there'd be little interest in the exercise either. Similarly, versions 2, 3 and 4 each come with implications. What we're trying to do here is use the Happy Line to identify areas for trade-offs and improvements. The best line splits the Post-its into two batches of equal importance, to increase the number of available trade-offs for improvement. So versions 3 or 4 in the illustration below are the most useful.

Drawing the Happy Line

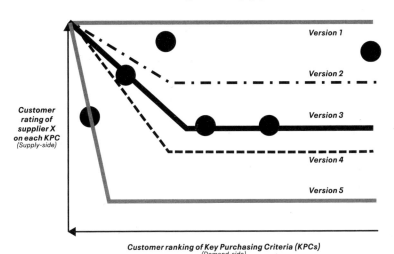

Customer rating of supplier X on each KPC *(Supply-side)*

Version 1
Version 2
Version 3
Version 4
Version 5

Customer ranking of Key Purchasing Criteria (KPCs)
(Demand-side)

Now that we've clarified where the line goes, let's talk about the three zones on the graph: Front, Top and Back. Each has its unique characteristics. The Front zone is the bottom left of the graph. It's the zone with criteria that really matter to customers, and on which supplier X is not perfect. Supplier X needs to focus the bulk of their ideas generation efforts on improving on the criteria in the Front zone. The Front zone is typically where the most strategic problems lie.

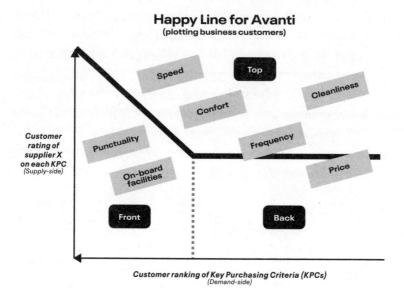

Happy Line for Avanti
(plotting business customers)

Customer ranking of Key Purchasing Criteria (KPCs)
(Demand-side)

In the case of the imaginary Avanti example, the team believed that the most important KPCs for business travellers were punctuality, then onboard facilities, then speed, then comfort, then frequency, then cleanliness, then price. By the way, that's usually a good way to present it. First go left to right, and then bottom to top. So the team believes that on punctuality Avanti is average, on onboard facilities slightly below average, on speed pretty good, on comfort pretty good, on frequency just above average, on cleanliness great, and on price a bit expensive.

Once you have these Post-its in position, irrespective of where the Happy Line bends specifically, you can see that there are two Post-its – punctuality and onboard facilities – that could be below most variants of the line. That's the Front zone, and you have to come up here with multiple ideas to increase punctuality and onboard facilities.

The second step is to tap into the Top zone. Let's look at some criteria that don't matter that much to customers, but where we're doing quite well. By preference, we would rather not touch them. Do you see that cleanliness appears not that important to customers, but we're doing very well? You can work out that if we were worse on cleanliness nothing good would come out of that. Also, achieving great cleanliness is not that expensive compared to terrible cleanliness, so let's leave it there. On things like comfort and frequency, however, business customers tell us we're good to excellent, and they don't care about it that much – punctuality and onboard facilities are much more important to them. So what do we do here? We come up with many ideas where we accept to trade off comfort and frequency as a way to improve punctuality and onboard facilities. For example, reducing frequency. This would lead to fewer trains circulating on the tracks, which might improve punctuality. Can you spot more ideas? Yes? Great. We'll see quite a few more shortly.

Finally, there is the Back zone. These are the criteria that don't matter that much, and we're not great at them. Here, again, you try to come up with ideas to improve things, but without compromising on any of the more important criteria.

In my experience, when people do a Happy Line in practice, they commonly spend way too long arriving at the Post-its, and way too little time extracting the insights. My suggestion is to swap around the usual time allocation. Spend five to 10 minutes plotting the Post-its, then spend 50 to 55 minutes extracting and packaging ideas. Once you are done, you'll have quite a few really good customer-centric ideas on how to fix the strategy for your business, department, team, or for yourself. These come from an appreciation of customers' needs and expectations.

In order to extract all the ideas contained in the Happy Line, I suggest you take a methodological approach, starting with '1-Post-it' ideas, before moving on to '2-Post-its' ideas, '3-Post-its' ideas, and so on.

A '1-Post-it' idea is an idea that would end up moving one Post-it higher, closer to the line. For example, 'incentivize train drivers to show up on time'. If implemented, this idea would improve average punctuality (if slightly), while leaving all the other Post-its in the same place. Likewise, 'invest in better signals on the track' is a '1-Post-it' idea. Please note that the new signals might help increase speed too, but that benefit would take the speed Post-it higher above the line, which is not what we want, hence the 'invest in signals' idea is a '1-Post-it' idea, and not a '2-Post-its' idea.

A '2-Post-its' idea is, unsurprisingly, an idea that results in two Post-its both getting closer to the line. For example, 'fewer trains daily' is a '2-Post-its' idea, as it increases punctuality by decreasing frequency and the crowding on the track. The more important KPC is improved (its Post-it goes up) while the less important KPC is compromised (its Post-it goes down).

On the whole, the more Post-its in an idea, the more subtle the idea (it has more moving parts), the less obvious the idea (it's more complicated), and the more likely it is to work (since an idea with multiple Post-its is the result of trade-offs between more KPCs).

Combining three Post-its, then four, then five or more to generate ideas becomes ever harder. But it is absolutely worth it. The best way to get there is to treat idea generation like a physical activity, and warm up with a comprehensive list of the easier '1-Post-it' and '2-Post-its' ideas first, and then progress on to three, four, etc.

Before spending time extracting all the ideas contained on a Happy Line framework, many people want to be sure they've got the correct Happy Line to start with. One way to do that is to go for a huge market research exercise, to find out if the line that you hypothesized (or the Post-it positions that you hypothesized) is indeed the one that customers endorse. I have a better suggestion for you, though.

Once you've done your first Happy Line, which was the result of a team effort (Persons 1 to 6), allow each member of the team to have a go at their own version of the diagnostic on a different flipchart. Each person on their own might arrive at a slightly different order of KPCs, horizontally, or vertically, or even different KPCs altogether. If they do it quickly, you can end up with many different versions of the Happy Line at speed.

The art of good teamwork is then to go through each version of the diagnostic in turn, and ask yourselves together, 'If this version X is correct, what ideas does it generate?' Since every version of the diagnostic will be slightly different, you'll end up with many more ideas than if you had only stayed with the initial team version. More surprisingly, perhaps, you will be taken aback by how many of your ideas are common to all versions, in spite of the difference in diagnostic between them. There is a simple reason for this: good ideas address many problems at once, and so can appear on many flipcharts at once.

It's important to note that usually no real data is used in a Happy Line exercise, and yet the ideas obtained are real ideas. Why? Because **you don't need real data to have real ideas!** In the balance of the two, a great solution trumps an accurate diagnostic all the time. So you won't solve your problem if you have a great diagnostic, but are bad at extracting ideas. Better to plot the Happy Line(s) very quickly, as a team and individually, and then take your time extracting ideas.

Generating all these ideas might take you an hour. You then have two choices, once the hour has elapsed: go ahead with that huge market research exercise we mentioned earlier (to confirm your initial diagnostic), or spend the same amount of cash testing your best ideas on your customers and/or other stakeholders. The choice is yours. I would always rather trust what customers do than what they say. And in a business context, I would always spend more money testing some solutions than on validating the original diagnostic.

The Happy Line in practice

The instructions below are for a typical 60-minute session, for three or four people.

> **Set the Scene** (1 min)
> Take a flipchart page, portrait, and split it in two. Draw the Happy Line axis in the top half (but *not* the Lazy-L shape), then draw four quadrants in the bottom half, with the numbers 1, 2, 3 and 4+). Choose the stakeholder X, from whose point of view you're approaching the issue (customers, employees, suppliers, etc.).

> **Assess Stakeholder X** (10 mins)
> Write down 10 to 12 KPCs on Post-its for this stakeholder X. Rank the KPCs in decreasing order along the horizontal axis, keeping only the top seven or eight, and letting the others 'fall out'. Rate the performance of the entity against these KPCs (as stakeholder X would). Draw the Happy Line(s) in a way that best allows you to generate interesting ideas (i.e.

retaining the Lazy-L shape and broadly splitting the Post-its evenly). Identify the KPCs with letters (a, b, c, etc.) in each bottom right corner of the Post-its.

> **Generate Ideas** (30 mins)
> Invent three or four ideas that improve the most critical KPC, and write them in Box 1. Come up with three or four ideas that move two Post-its and write them in Box 2. Continue with '3-Post-its' ideas and '4-Post-its' ideas, etc. Use Post-its of a different colour, and write in brackets the letters of the KPC your idea is altering, for ease of understanding by others of the trade-off you envisage. For example, 'Bla bla bla (a g f).'

> **Package Your Best Ideas** (15 mins)
> Summarize your best ideas in two to four words each, using words that convey them crisply and clearly (and add the unique component letters that triggered the idea, for clarity).

> **Repeat for Stakeholders Y, Z, etc.** (as necessary).

Here are four additional tips on how to use the Happy Line in practice.

> **Tip 1:** When trying to fit the initial 10 to 12 KPCs you thought of into the seven or eight you are plotting, don't merge two high-importance KPCs into one. Most strategic thinking contains a fair amount of clustering (i.e. grouping together things that go together). It is important to resist this urge when plotting KPCs. If anything, take the opposite view, and always check if any of the top four or five KPCs contain one or more smaller ones. If the latter on their own are important enough to make it into the top seven, then they deserve to be spun off.

Stakeholder X

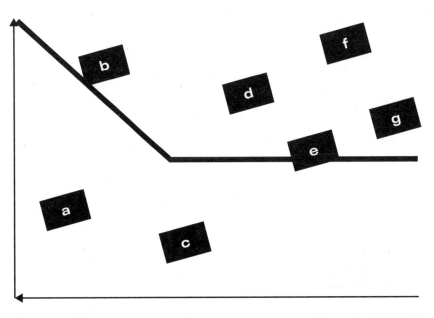

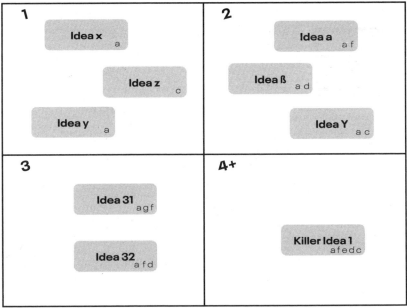

> **Tip 2:** There's a handy way to remember whether the idea you've generated is legitimate or not: it should make the Post-its move clockwise. You want the criteria in the Front zone to improve (i.e. Post-its go up on the left) while the ones in the Top zone are slightly compromised (i.e. Post-its go down on the right).

> **Tip 3:** The first idea people come up with is often 'improve A'. This can usually be followed by at least five or six more specific ways to achieve that desired improvement in A. The more specific the idea, the better.

> **Tip 4:** With '3-Post-its' or '4-Post-its' ideas it is getting difficult to write the idea in full on its own Post-it at the bottom of the chart. That's where the lettering of the top Post-its helps. Instead of labelling an idea 'have less frequent trains to help lessen the congestion on the track and therefore increase punctuality' you can write 'one less train daily (a, e)'. Since (a) relates to punctuality in our example and (e) relates to frequency, writing '(a, e)' after the 'one less train daily' clarifies the shift in the top Post-its that the idea delivers.

Happy Line exercise:
How to make your boss happy?

The Happy Line is a technique for visualizing the relationship between two parties, and finding ways to optimize it. It clearly works well in a business context, between a company and its customers. It can also be applied between a company and its suppliers, its regulator, its shareholders, etc. Or even between a department (IT, HR, finance, etc.) and its internal clients (marketing, sales, finance, etc.).

In a different context, the Happy Line works brilliantly too as a way to get along better with your parents, your siblings, your romantic partner, or anyone who has expectations from you, or has a personal relationship with you. Naturally, the Happy Line is perfectly suited to finding new and better ways to satisfy that most critical stakeholder:

your immediate boss. So how should you use the Happy Line to improve your relationship with your boss?

First, ask yourself, 'What's important to my boss, in a direct report?' Then rank these criteria on the horizontal axis, by decreasing order of importance to your boss (most important criteria on the left, always, getting less important from left to right). For the vertical plotting, ask yourself, 'How well would my boss say I'm doing on these dimensions if I asked him or her?' Have a hypothesis yourself, based on the feedback you may have received already – past praise and criticisms are both good clues to what matters to your boss, and how you've been faring so far.

As you know by now, once you have a diagnostic in place, go through the '1-Post-it', '2-Post-its', etc. routine to come up with ideas to optimize your relationship with your boss. Next, start doing some of these new things. If your boss responds positively, it was a good idea – whether your diagnostic was correct or not. If your boss doesn't respond positively, then you need to try alternative ideas and/or redo your diagnostic.

From experience, three out of four initiatives are positively received, and the other one is usually not even noticed by the boss. The Happy Line approach is a very strategic technique for accelerating your career! Do practise with the following two exercises, and share your results on www.strategic.how/happy:

> **Happy Line exercise #1**
  identify better ideas to improve the interactions between
  Phil and his boss.

> **Happy Line exercise #2**
  plot the Happy Line diagnostic between you and your boss,
  and come up with at least five ideas that will make him or
  her happier.

HAPPY LINE EXERCISE #1:
PHIL VS HIS BOSS

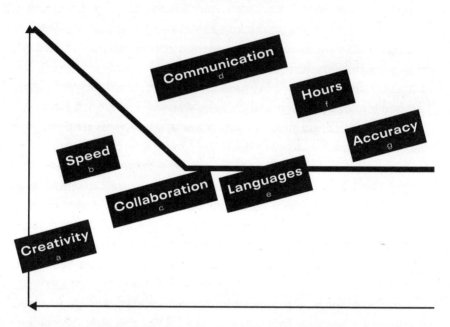

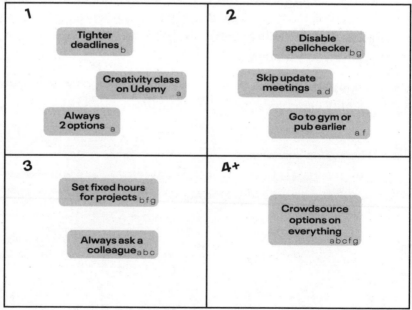

HAPPY LINE EXERCISE #2:
YOU VS YOUR BOSS

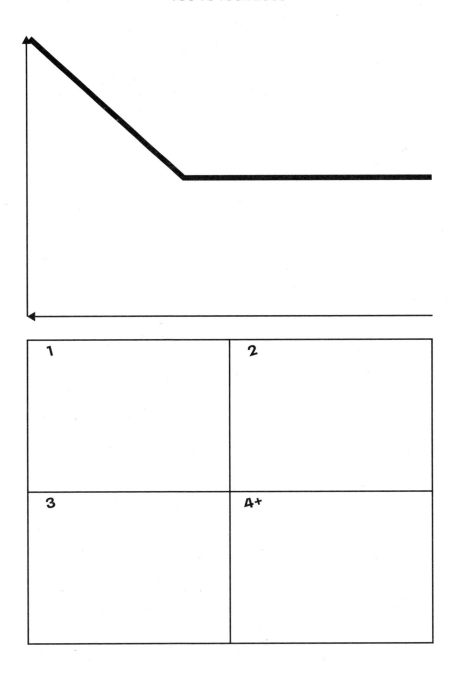

4.

MUTATION GAME

Darwinism in business

What's the best way to come up with a great new idea in business? There are two time-honoured approaches that work really well.

The first one is to copy the competition. It's not smart, it's not big, it's not clever, but it works really well. Why? Because innovation fails. All studies suggest that the success of innovation is anywhere between 5 per cent and 20 per cent. Let's call that 10 per cent. If your competitor is doing something that you can see is working, you're now looking at the visible 10 per cent of the gigantic iceberg of innovation they've gone through: 90 per cent of what they tried has failed. Many people reckon you're better off just copying the one in 10 ideas of your competitors that have worked out, rather than creating your own iceberg of failure. I agree that keeping up with their successes is good, but adding other sources of inspiration is even better.

The second common way to come up with great ideas in business is therefore to ask customers. Or observe customers, or inspire yourself from customers. Starting from the demand side (customers), not the supply side (competitors). We've just seen how the Happy Line is a great way to turn a focus on customers into innovative ideas for success, via new products, new services, new processes, etc. The Happy Line markedly increases the likelihood of innovation success.

I now want to introduce a third angle. My suggestion to you is to mutate yourself. Instead of copying competitors or asking customers, mutating yourself starts from you. It comes from the organization you are today, with your capabilities, your customers, your competitors, your products, services, processes, etc. We look to tweak this ever so slightly, in the hope of achieving a step change in performance.

What is a mutation? In biology, a mutation is a small random variation in the genes. It's an error in the self-copying process. A mutation is the first step in a potentially useful evolution. Charles Darwin defines natural selection as the principle by which slight variation (aka mutation), if useful, is preserved. Mutation is the first step in natural selection. It's quite random, unpredictable, and yet essential.

In business, most practices are set to avoid errors and unpredictability at all costs. Repeating exactly the same thing every time is a highly valued aspect of industrial and professional competence. It's at the heart of widely adopted efficiency techniques like Six Sigma. In business, a mutation is seen as dangerous.

The Mutation Game challenges that fear, and flips it on its head. The Mutation Game is a way to intentionally replicate in a business context the characteristics and benefits of natural selection, applied to ideas rather than biological entities. We're going to artificially create a large number of mutations in a business object (process, product, industry, etc.), and see which ones survive the best.

FOUR SIMPLE STEPS FOR PLAYING THE MUTATION GAME

1. Write a short sentence that describes the business object you want to mutate (whether it's a process, a product, an industry, etc.).
2. List a couple of variants for each component in the sentence.
3. String together different variants to create mutations.
4. Spark many new ideas off these multiple mutations.

Let's see that in practice. For example, close your eyes and picture the reception area at your company. Now think of five to eight words that you could cobble together in a sentence to describe it, and the associated reception process. We're trying to make sure that each word in the sentence is meaningful, so we avoid too many bridging words ('and', 'the', etc.).

Here would be my suggestion to you. A typical reception area – or reception process, to be more specific – can be described as: '**two people** | **sitting** | **behind desks** | **welcoming** | **colleagues'** | **visitors**'.

What we have here are six components – six sets of genes, if you want – that describe the current reception process. We're going to mutate the whole process by generating variants for each component.

For example, the first component is 'two people'. What else could we have instead? We could have 'one person', or 'nobody', or 'a few people', or 'everyone'. Instead of 'sitting', we could have 'standing', 'walking', etc. At this point we're not passing judgement, we're just listing logical alternatives to the current component. If we go with the next one, 'behind desks', we could have 'in front of desks', 'on desks', 'in the open', etc. Then instead of 'welcoming' we could have 'turning away', 'ushering in', 'registering', etc. For 'colleagues', we could have 'own' or 'anyone's', and for 'visitors' we might have 'deliveries' or 'vehicles'.

Let's pause for a second here. From experience, whenever I run these sessions live with an audience, by the third or fourth component in the sentence, people start coming up with slightly silly ideas ('on desks', 'turning away', etc.). It's absolutely fine! It's a great way to explore the richness of variants available to you.

Mutating the Reception Process

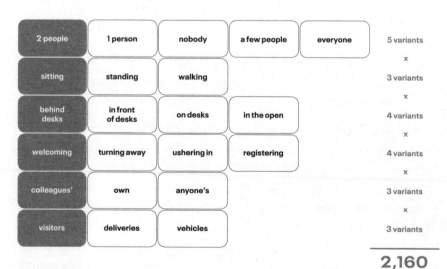

2 people	1 person	nobody	a few people	everyone	5 variants
					x
sitting	standing	walking			3 variants
					x
behind desks	in front of desks	on desks	in the open		4 variants
					x
welcoming	turning away	ushering in	registering		4 variants
					x
colleagues'	own	anyone's			3 variants
					x
visitors	deliveries	vehicles			3 variants

2,160
MUTATIONS

How many potential mutations for the reception process have we created at this point? Well, we've got five variants for the number of people, three variants for their position, four variants on their location, etc. When you multiply them together, you realize that we've just created 2,160 potential mutations of the reception process (i.e. 2,160 different ways to create a new sentence by picking one component per row in the grid above).

Not all of the potential mutations contained in this grid will prove useful, so not all of them will survive natural selection. In order to increase our odds, let's first eliminate some of the variants we sort of know are not going to work out. Let's put 'on desks' in the bin, 'turning away' in the bin, 'registering' is actually part of welcoming, etc. What we end up with is five variants for the number of people, three for their position, etc. Multiply these, and you realize that we still have 90 potential mutations available to us in the new grid: 90 different ways to combine elements together creatively to invent different versions of our reception process (aka mutating it).

Mutating the Reception Process

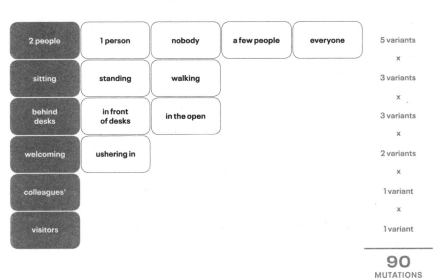

2 people	1 person	nobody	a few people	everyone	5 variants
					x
sitting	standing	walking			3 variants
					x
behind desks	in front of desks	in the open			3 variants
					x
welcoming	ushering in				2 variants
					x
colleagues'					1 variant
					x
visitors					1 variant

90
MUTATIONS

The proportion of these 90 mutations that will turn out to prove useful is probably a lot higher than in the 2,160 mutations we started out with. It's always good to come up with a large grid, to stimulate creativity, and then to shrink it back a bit, like we've just done, to ensure a high ratio of practical ideas.

Let's have a look at some of these 90 potential mutations in detail to see if a few might indeed prove useful and survive testing. A first one might be: 'one person | sitting | behind desks | welcoming | colleagues' | visitors'.

Mutating the Reception Process

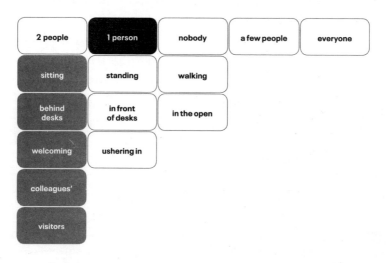

Only one component has changed between the original description of the reception process and the mutation we're examining here. From 'two people' to 'one person'. What would we have to change in the real world for this mutation to prove useful? Add more beanbags in the lobby. Or sofas, or seats. Because, effectively, when you go from 'two people' to 'one person' sitting behind desks welcoming colleagues' visitors, you haven't changed much. You will save costs, but you will create slightly longer queues in your lobby at critical moments in the day. It's probably cheaper for the company who runs the reception area. It's a bit more painful for the visitors. You have to decide whether saving a few pounds is worth the hassle for your visitors, or vice versa. The new process is a slight mutation of the old one. The difference in nature is tiny (one less receptionist), but the difference in outcome (cost, speed, decor) might be enormous.

Let's look at a slightly more radical mutation, with: '**nobody | sitting | behind desks | welcoming | colleagues' | visitors**'. Could that be a useful mutation and, if so, what would the new reception process look like in practice?

Mutating the Reception Process

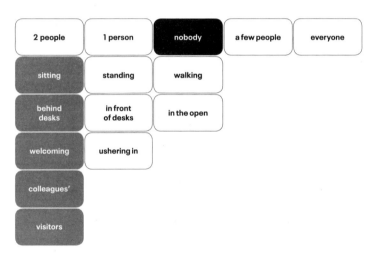

In this instance, our new reception process could be a virtual receptionist. A touchscreen in the middle of the lobby area, where visitors identify themselves, and their host is alerted to their presence by text or email. This solution is becoming ever more common, and the mutation that gave birth to it is clearly worth retaining.

Now, how about '**everyone | walking | in the open | welcoming | colleagues' | visitors**'. We have here a combination of words that's a little bit more puzzling.

The thinking has to be, either, this is a silly way to combine things because it's been created automatically, or yes, it's been created automatically but, because it appears less logical than other options, it forces us to envisage possible solutions that we haven't thought of before.

Mutating the Reception Process

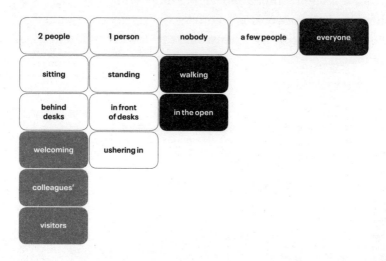

How would we describe this reception area, or this reception process? Oh, of course. That's like the Apple Store. The Apple Store is built that way. So, the Apple Store layout is a mutation of the typical reception process. This mutation has proved useful, and has therefore been retained. So, the Apple Store layout can be thought of as a result of natural selection applied to the reception process.

Let's do one more. How about 'one person | standing | in front of desks | ushering in | colleagues' | visitors'. This is a mutation with four differences from the original description of the reception process. And what would that give us?

Yes indeed, it's something like a restaurant-style approach. What does that mean in practice? I don't really know just yet, because it's not as easy to picture and label as 'Apple Store' was a second ago, where everyone understood the meaning right away.

Here, we've created a mutation of the reception process that feels a bit like a maître d' at a restaurant, but we haven't quite understood what it means in practice yet. That's great. That's what the Mutation Game does. It helps you open up new possibilities. Either possibilities that are immediately easy to picture, label and apply (for example, the Apple Store) or possibilities that feel more difficult to put words to, even if they feel interesting (for example, the maître d').

Mutating the Reception Process

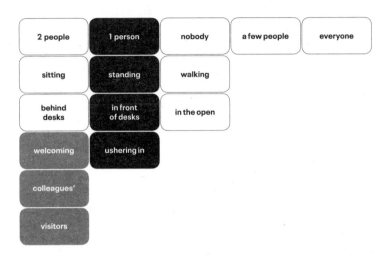

The aim of the Mutation Game is to change little in the description of a business object (product, process, industry, etc.) while achieving a big change on the outside. If you can clearly see the link between your new version of the description and the original one, then it's likely you won't find it too hard to implement the ideas triggered by this new version. On the other hand, these new ideas could appeal massively to your audience (customers, boss, colleagues, etc.). Minimal changes on the inside, for maximum impact on the outside.

Another huge benefit of the Mutation Game is that it is entirely words-based. No complex maths or finance are used in this technique. Everyone in the company can play. At every level, in every function, on every issue. The Mutation Game is a great thinking technique in that it can extract new ideas from the brain of every single person in the company, on every single issue you face, without the need for expensive training or additional resources. A few Posts-its and a wall will do. You are generating dozens of great ideas quickly.

Mutation Game examples and exercises

Let's look at an example about mutating the taxi industry. In most cities, you can probably use a sentence to describe the traditional taxi industry as follows: '**individuals | hailing | in the street | random | licensed taxis | for a short ride**'.

You know what happens next. We're going to look at each of the components of the sentence, and come up with variants. Instead of 'individuals' we might say 'groups' or 'objects'. Instead of 'hailing' we might come up with 'booking ahead'. 'In the street' could become 'on the phone' or 'online'. 'Random' might become 'known' or 'approved'. 'Licensed taxis' could become 'unlicensed taxis' or 'private drivers'. 'For a short ride', 'for a long ride'. We end up with 324 potential mutations in this grid.

Mutating the Taxi Industry

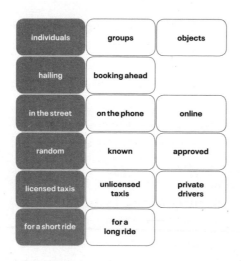

individuals	groups	objects	3 variants
			x
hailing	booking ahead		2 variants
			x
in the street	on the phone	online	3 variants
			x
random	known	approved	3 variants
			x
licensed taxis	unlicensed taxis	private drivers	3 variants
			x
for a short ride	for a long ride		2 variants

324
MUTATIONS

There are only six components in our original description. That's very compact. And we limit ourselves to two or three variants per component. That's nothing. Yet we still arrive, in under a minute, at 324 possible ways to transform the taxi industry – and that's a staggering amount. Let's take a look at a few of these mutations.

Mutating the Taxi Industry

individuals	groups	objects
hailing	**booking ahead**	
in the street	**on the phone**	online
random	known	approved
licensed taxis	unlicensed taxis	private drivers
for a short ride	for a long ride	

For example, if we go 'individuals | booking ahead | on the phone | random | licenced taxis | for a short ride'. In Britain, that would be minicabs. Every country probably has its own version of this.

If you go one step further, and since we're now 'booking ahead' and 'on the phone', then we can go to 'private drivers' rather than 'licensed taxis', and 'approved' instead of 'random', and what we now have is 'individuals | booking ahead | on the phone | approved | private drivers | for a short ride'. That's Uber, Lyft, Didi, etc., and a lot of other well-known apps in the ride-hailing space.

Let's look at other aspects of mutating the taxi industry that are available for us, should we be able to spot them – or might have been profitably available to us, had we been able to spot them a few years ago – by changing different components. Let's vary the bottom two rows in the grid, and check out: 'individuals | hailing | in the street | random | private drivers | for a long ride'.

You can easily spot that this is hitchhiking. Possibly a dying art form of transport in developed economies, but still a very popular one all around the world.

Mutating the Taxi Industry

Mutating the Taxi Industry

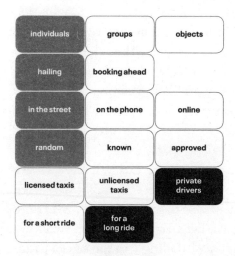

Let's vary even more rows, and go more extreme, with '**individuals | booking ahead | online | approved | private drivers | for a long ride**'.

Because more of the rows are different from the starting description, we know the idea that will result is going to be quite different from the traditional taxi industry. Those of you in the know might recognize BlaBlaCar. Those of you not in the know might nevertheless have spotted that this combination of components feels full of potential. A halfway house between hitchhiking and bus services.

Mutating the Taxi Industry

When you look at the ideas we have come up with, one idea is worth several dozen billion dollars (Uber), another is worth several billion dollars (BlaBlaCar) and one is worth nothing (hitchhiking).

The Mutation Game approach works well to come up with new processes, as we've seen for the reception area process, but also new companies, as we've just seen with the taxi industry. It also works well to come up with new initiatives, new products, new businesses, new industries, etc. The Mutation Game is a universally applicable way to go 'Up' in your thinking, early on in projects. It helps you come up very quickly with a wide range of options that might work. We'll see later, in 'Down', how to select the best of these ideas to arrive at a workable new solution.

Mutating Peter's Social Life

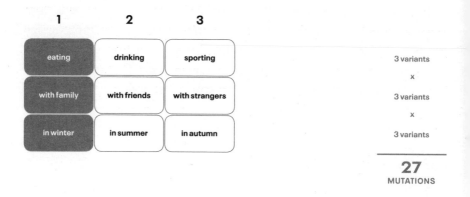

Let me invite you now to carry out a quick and simple exercise, to get a better feel for the whole process. Imagine that Peter is an old American friend of yours who happens to be a bit dissatisfied with his social life at the moment. When asked to describe his social life, he replied: '**eating | with family | in winter**'. Clearly, Thanksgiving, Christmas and the Super Bowl have taken over Peter's social life, and it's time to add some novelty in there. What's the best way to change things a tiny bit on the inside in order to achieve a large change in outcome on the outside? The Mutation Game! Let's mutate Peter's social life.

Grab a pen and paper, and list as many ideas as come to your mind using the three rows in the grid above. We've kept the grid small, with only two alternatives for each component. How many ideas can you come up with, in addition to Thanksgiving, Christmas or Boxing Day? We've numbered the columns above to help you give a unique number to each mutation and keep track of your ideas. For example, 'barbecue' would be an idea that comes from mutation 112 ('**eating | with family | in summer**'), and 'festival' would come from mutation 232 ('**drinking | with strangers | in summer**'). Because we only have a very small number of possible mutations in this exercise (27 instead of the thousands in a typical case), we can put these in a table.

Mutating Peter's Social Life

MUTATIONS			MUTATION UNIQUE NUMBER	IDEAS
eating	with family	in winter	111	Christmas dinner, Thanksgiving
eating	with family	in summer	112	Barbecue, picnic in the park
eating	with family	in autumn	113	...
eating	with friends	in winter	121	Raclette evening
eating	with friends	in summer	122	...
eating	with friends	in autumn	123	Country walk and pub lunch
eating	with strangers	in winter	131	...
eating	with strangers	in summer	132	etc
eating	with strangers	in autumn	133	
drinking	with family	in winter	211	
drinking	with family	in summer	212	
drinking	with family	in autumn	213	
drinking	with friends	in winter	221	
drinking	with friends	in summer	222	
drinking	with friends	in autumn	223	
drinking	with strangers	in winter	231	
drinking	with strangers	in summer	232	
drinking	with strangers	in autumn	233	
sporting	with family	in winter	311	
sporting	with family	in summer	312	
sporting	with family	in autumn	313	
sporting	with friends	in winter	321	
sporting	with friends	in summer	322	
sporting	with friends	in autumn	323	
sporting	with strangers	in winter	331	
sporting	with strangers	in summer	332	
sporting	with strangers	in autumn	333	

The table is incomplete on purpose, and you should feel free to add the ideas you've just discovered on your own. In my experience, people run out of steam on their own after eight or 10 ideas, which is why it's good to play the Mutation Game with a few other people (typically four to six).

You'll notice in the table that one mutation can trigger more than one idea. Mutation 112 can make you think of both a barbecue and a picnic in the park. Likewise, one idea can come from several different mutations. A country walk and pub lunch can be thought of as both an eating idea (from mutation 123) or a sporting idea (from mutation 323). This is absolutely fine, and actually desirable. The more mutations you explore, the more likely you are to come up with great ideas.

Remember, natural selection is the process by which a mutation, if useful, is preserved. The more mutations you explore, the more likely it becomes that one of them will prove useful. What does that mean in our exercise? It means going through as many of the 27 mutations as you can cope with, and forcing yourself to have as many ideas as possible. It's easy to realize that the more ideas you have, the more likely it becomes that two or three of these will radically transform Peter's social life.

The Mutation Game in practice

The instructions below are for a typical 60-minute session, with four to six people. The Mutation Game can be run well with just Post-its, marker pens and a wall. You should also check out our app at www.strategic.how/mutation for a more productive session.

> **Craft a Description** (5 mins)
  Pick a meaningful string of five to eight components that describe in one sentence the object to mutate as it stands today. Put these components on Post-its in a column. (One word per component is the ideal scenario. A component can still contain more than one word, when appropriate, for example, 'for a short ride'.)

> **Generate Alternative Components** (15 mins)
  Generate a grid of alternative components, with two to four alternatives for each of the components in the initial description sentence (if need be, by writing five or six alternatives and then choosing your preferred ones).

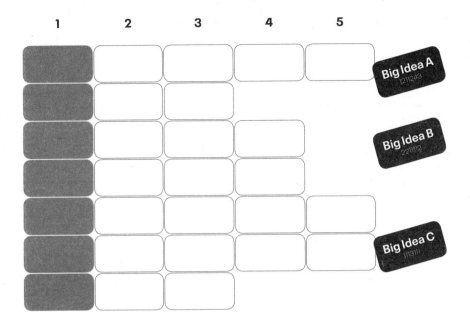

> **Pick Mutations and Generate Ideas** (30 mins)
>
> A mutation is a sentence arrived at by selecting one Post-it per row. Each mutation gets a unique number, made by listing the column numbers of the words it contains. (NB: the mutation number of the initial description is a long string of '1s'.) Go through around 50 mutations, spending 10 to 20 seconds per mutation, to trigger creative ideas. You can have more than one idea per mutation, and many mutations can give rise to the same idea. Move on to another mutation if you find yourself drawing a blank at any time.

> **Package your Best Ideas** (10 mins)
>
> Summarize your best ideas in two to four words each, to convey them crisply and clearly (and add the unique mutation number of the mutation that triggered the idea, for recollection).

Here are four additional tips on how to use the Mutation Game in practice.

> **Tip 1:** Aim for a rectangular grid. The perfect shape of grid for the game is probably five to eight components vertically, and two to four alternatives horizontally. As much as possible, try to fill in the grid to the full extent of the rectangle (i.e. fewer blank spaces than in the reception process example).

> **Tip 2:** Start with only one or two variants when examining the mutations. The closer a mutation is to the original description, the more likely it will be to trigger ideas that make sense. If you pick too many rows with a component other than the original one, you're more likely to get wild ideas . . . or nothing. Starting to examine mutations by picking everything from the right side of the grid for a few minutes is a great way to loosen the inhibitions and kick-start the creative juices. Returning to the left to pick most components will yield easier ideas that are more likely to survive the test of reality in due course.

> **Tip 3:** Prefer an original description that starts with the demand side, but try both. In the taxi example, our original description started with the demand side, as 'individuals hailing . . .', whereas a supply-led description would be something like 'experienced drivers roaming the street in search of passengers for a short ride'. Demand-led and supply-led descriptions offer different benefits, and both should be tried. Starting with the demand side usually expands the mind more – and the customer is king!

> **Tip 4:** Use the app at www.strategic.how/mutation. There are two key benefits of using the app over the Post-its-and-wall version. The first one is the sheer quantity of mutations that you can go through in the app, thanks to the 'save and review' functionality. You can check mutations at speed, a bit like on Tinder, and swipe left to save the ones you'd like to spend a bit more time with later. The other benefit is the ability to truly randomize the mutations. When picking a mutation by hand, you will be tempted to craft a meaningful sentence as you go down from row to row – in other words,

you will unconsciously skew the choice. The app instead allows you to properly test yourself against surprisingly random mutations, which usually lead to more significant breakthroughs and innovation. The app is closer to true natural selection than the Post-its-and-wall version of the game!

Mutation Game exercise:
How to diversify McKinsey?

The Mutation Game is a divergent thinking technique that helps create thousands of alternatives to anything, in the blink of an eye.

Let's pretend here that the senior team at McKinsey Brazil is looking for ways to diversify. We could also be the senior team at BCG Japan, or Monitor Deloitte Italy, etc. Anywhere where the economy in the country has been flat for the last few years, the competition from other strategy consulting firms is intensifying, and a senior team might want to explore the boundaries of their business, to see if some contiguous areas might offer richer pickings.

The first step is to write a sentence, of five to eight words, describing the object one seeks to mutate: in this case, their consulting business. Most objects to mutate can be described from both the supply side and the demand side. Here are four attempts to write a sentence describing the consulting business, two from each side.

> **Demand:** one | firm | paying | external | professionals | to deliver | projects
> **Demand:** companies | receiving | advice | on issues | from | qualified | people
> **Supply:** people | helping | clients | solve | difficult | business | challenges
> **Supply:** experts | helping | clients | solve | business | problems | for a fee

Whenever you've settled on a sentence, you then fill out a grid of alternative components, with two to four alternatives for each of the components in the sentence. Once you're happy with your grid, go through around 50 possible mutations at speed, to trigger new ideas. You can then summarize your best ideas in two to four words each, with the unique mutation number attached to facilitate understanding.

We have two exercises for you to practise your Mutation Game skills now, and we invite you to share your solutions on www.strategic. how/mutation:

> **Mutation Game exercise #1**
identify better ideas to diversify McKinsey Brazil that can be derived from Haruto's sentence and grid.

> **Mutation Game exercise #2**
craft an alternative sentence, with your own grid, and at least three ideas that could help diversify McKinsey Brazil.

MUTATION GAME EXERCISE #1:
HARUTO'S TAKE ON DIVERSIFYING MCKINSEY BRAZIL

| | | | Management Consulting 113121 | Best-Practice Forum 414152 | TripAdvisor for Business 211112 | Alert Service 323114 |

	1	2	3	4	5
	Experts	consumers	AI	clients	contractors
	Helping	researching	reviewing	sharing	inventing
	Clients	employees	competitors	shareholders	society
	Solve	clarify	implement	test	mitigate
	Business	industry	societal	personal	political
	Problems	solutions	ideas	opportunities	methods
	For a fee	for free	in exchange	by subscription	for a hug

MUTATION GAME EXERCISE #2:
YOUR TAKE ON DIVERSIFYING MCKINSEY BRAZIL

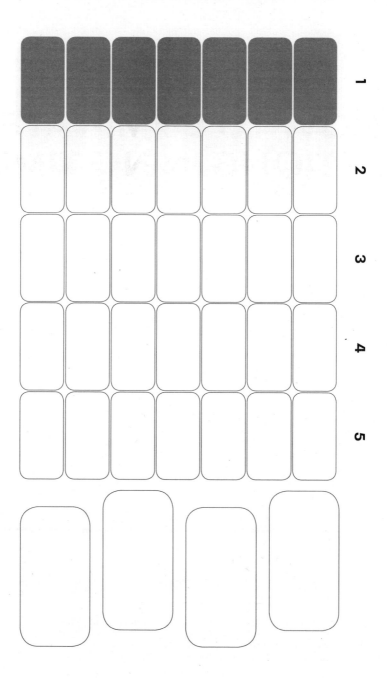

PART THREE

HOW TO ELIMINATE OPTIONS IN NO TIME ('DOWN')

There are many ways to get from Clarity to Certainty in a business context, and we mentioned in **How to Solve Complex Problems** ('Think') that you could:

> - employ various **qualitative techniques** to pit all your ideas against one another, and have the ideas themselves create their own ranking
> - apply some of the many **quantitative techniques** available to offer a more numerically derived validation of your options to date, and
> - construct **real-life tests**, whenever possible, to demonstrate in practice the viability or otherwise of each of your remaining options.

In this part, **How to Eliminate Options in No Time** ('Down'), we'll go over one technique from each family:

> - a **qualitative technique**, the **Payoff Profiles Matrix**
> - a **quantitative technique**, with **Landscape Analysis**, and
> - a **real-life test**, the **Lean Startup**.

Broadly speaking, the 'Down' techniques combine three weapons to destroy ideas: words, numbers, actions. If an idea sounds right (using words) and scores well (against numbers) and fares okay in practice (against small-scale tests), then it's probably one of the best ideas you have in your portfolio. Validating ideas requires an element of all three approaches, and probably in that order too. Words come easy and cost little, and numbers are not expensive but the right ones can take a while to appear. Real-life tests and actions are getting less and less expensive in many industries, but they can take longer to set up. And you want to make sure you're testing the best ideas to date. Hence the order: words, numbers, actions.

So 'Down' is about diving from a great height into the world of data (words, numbers, actions) to identify the likelihood that an idea you've already had will be successful, or not. Not uncommonly, data will prove sparse, unreliable and contradictory. Unsurprisingly, you might feel at that moment that you're further away from Completion than you've been since the start of the project. But there will be light at the end of that tunnel! It is also common on some projects to experience a proper rollercoaster ride, with more than one 'Up' swing to Clarity, and more than one 'Down' dive into the world of data. Eventually, you will reach Certainty that you have at hand as robust a proof for your idea(s) as you'll get.

Any good 'Down' session needs to combine the three techniques listed here. Be aware that the Payoff Profiles Matrix usually takes about an hour, Landscape Analysis can take a few hours to a few days, and Lean Startup can last from a few minutes to a few weeks.

5

PAYOFF PROFILES

The Payoff Profiles Matrix

One can easily think of a business as a portfolio of initiatives, or 'moves'. If a business is a portfolio of initiatives, then the higher the number of initiatives that turn out to be successful, the better the business will be doing. Success comes from managing well an ongoing portfolio of such 'moves'.

These 'moves' can be old projects, new ones, or even just some very recent twinkles in the eyes of your people. For example, brand-new ideas they've just had as a result of an 'Up' drive, along the lines we've seen in the previous chapters; typically, while using the Happy Line, the Mutation Game, or other recipes for generating great ideas quickly.

The Payoff Profiles Matrix is a fantastic way to quickly classify, prioritize and improve the 'moves' in your life. It works really well for big, company-wide projects, all the way down to team-specific initiatives. And that goes for people who don't like numbers, as well as for people who do like numbers . . . so that's the whole company covered.

We now need to introduce three notions: the Postures, the Bets and the Matrix itself.

THE POSTURES

Let's start with the Postures. At its most basic, a company (or a division, or a team) can choose to deal with the future in three different ways, and these three postures are:

> - shape the future
> - adapt to the future, or
> - reserve the right to play.

Companies like Apple typically seek to shape the future. Whatever they do, they try to achieve leadership in their industry, and win by playing a key role in setting the standards, creating the demand, etc. At the other end of the spectrum, reserving the right to play means investing sufficiently to stay in the game while avoiding premature commitments. One might argue that Microsoft has spent the last 20 years reserving the right to play across many fields, by investing a little bit to stay in various games (search with Bing, workplace chat with Teams, etc.).

Other companies might relentlessly choose to adapt to the future, and be the second-fastest mover in the market. They aim to win through speed, agility and flexibility in recognizing and capturing opportunities in existing markets. Deloitte, for example, has always been confident about arriving in markets only after others have already opened them up, and then trying to overtake them.

Finally, the vast majority of companies spread their initiatives across all three postures. They try to shape the future in some areas, adapt to it in others, and reserve the right to play in yet more.

THE BETS

Alongside these Postures, the second notion of interest to us here are the Bets that companies typically go for. In a business context, there are broadly three types of bets:

> 'no regret' moves,
> options, and
> big bets.

'No regret' moves are decisions that have a positive outcome in any scenario. Possibly a bit self-servingly, I tend to think of training as falling in that category. Investing in training always yields a positive payoff. Sometimes a little bit positive, sometimes very positive, and sometimes utterly transformational. Training is a 'no regret' move.

Options are typically bets that start with a small upfront payment. In most instances that spend yields nothing, or very little, and in a few instances, it pays big. A classic example of an option would be the lottery. You buy the ticket, and most of the time you just throw it in the bin. Every so often, though, you get something big in return.

The final type of bets are big bets; scenarios where, in some context, you get a really big positive payoff, and in others you get a big negative payoff. Imagine playing Russian roulette for money, with a loaded gun. Yes, you can win big, but you can also lose big; and you'd better know the odds before playing (i.e. how many bullets are left).

THE MATRIX

We can now combine Postures and Bets into a 3x3 grid. The resulting Payoff Profiles Matrix maps the different types of Bets companies can engage in against the different types of Postures they can adopt to deal with the future. The horizontal axis (Postures) reads shape-adapt-reserve from left to right, and the vertical axis (Bets) reads big bets-options-no regrets from top to bottom.

Payoff Profiles Matrix

	SHAPE	ADAPT	RESERVE
BIG BETS			
OPTIONS			
NO REGRETS			

Imagine that you are currently contemplating 10 to 20 initiatives, whether by the company as a whole, your business unit, your department or your team. We're now going to use a Post-it for each initiative, and plot all of them in the Matrix. Typical initiatives include 'enter market X', 'launch new product Y', 'move all communications to Slack', 'revamp the sales reward scheme', 'acquire company Z', 'reorganize the marketing function', 'redo the logo', etc.

We ask two questions to plot each initiative in turn:

> is this initiative a big bet, an option, or a 'no regret' move?
> does it shape the future, adapt to it, or reserve the right to play?

Depending on the number of participants in the room, positioning the Post-its can be a bit time-consuming, with many a debate. As a rule, go quickly through the initiatives first, and plot right away the ones on whose positioning there is full agreement. Do a second round, more slowly, for those initiatives that are subject to debate. Comparing with the initiatives already positioned will help. The Payoff Profiles Matrix summarizes visually your company as a portfolio of initiatives, as in the illustration below, and helps you optimize this portfolio through four key decisions: delegate, destroy, discuss or drag.

Payoff Profiles of the Initiatives

	SHAPE	ADAPT	RESERVE
BIG BETS	▪▪	▪ ▪	▪▪ ▪
OPTIONS	▪▪	▪	▪
NO REGRETS	▪		▪

Delegate

The first decision is to Delegate the 'no regret' moves. You remove these initiatives from the grid right away. These initiatives are typically something that the participants in the room shouldn't be discussing. By definition, a 'no regret' move is an initiative whose payoff is going to be positive. Delegate it, and let your juniors make a name for themselves by achieving the biggest payoff they can.

Payoff Profiles and the Decisions

	SHAPE	ADAPT	RESERVE
BIG BETS			
OPTIONS			
NO REGRETS	DELEGATE		

Destroy

The second decision is to Destroy the 'reserve big bets', in the top right corner of the grid. That corner should be absolutely empty. There is no reason for a company to take a big bet while only reserving the right to play. Why? Because the vertical axis in the Matrix is, broadly speaking, a measure of risk, and the horizontal axis is, broadly speaking, a measure of reward. The Payoff Profiles Matrix is a risk–reward matrix by another name. 'Reserve big bets' initiatives present way too much risk for the reward they offer. What is to be done? Improve the payoff. Alter the current version of the initiative into a new version, whose payoff profile will be positioned in a more optimal part of the Matrix.

Payoff Profiles and the Decisions

	SHAPE	ADAPT	RESERVE
BIG BETS		? ←	DESTROY
OPTIONS		? ↙	? ↓
NO REGRETS	DELEGATE		

There are three ways to improve the payoff profile of a 'reserve big bet' initiative. If we're going to stay with this amount of risk, we should move the initiative towards 'adapt'. In other words, can we do something that brings greater benefits to the company? Alternatively, we might decide that if we're just reserving the right to play, we should move the initiative towards 'options'. In other words, can we split it into successive stages that we invest in only once the first ones have worked out? Even better, let's try to combine both shifts by concocting a new version of the current initiative that is both less risky (option rather than big bet) and more rewarding (adapt rather than reserve)?

For example, a big initiative of both Facebook and Google is their attempt to circle the Earth with high-altitude objects to expand internet coverage. Google's Project Loon was unveiled in 2013 as a very ambitious bet to bring the internet to the whole world via a global array of balloons. This was clearly a 'big bet reserve' in that the probability and costs of failure were very high, and even in the case of success, the achieved outcome might not be that different to what could be achieved by other means (i.e. just one more way to deliver internet services to people).

What are the ways to improve Project Loon and move it away from its 'big bet reserve' position? There are three possibilities:

> ▸ down to 'options' (for example, by launching only one balloon at a time)
> ▸ left to 'adapt' (for example, by focusing on a country without much internet coverage)
> ▸ down and left (by launching just one balloon in one country).

As it turns out, Loon announced in July 2018 its first commercial deal: partnering with Telkom Kenya to deliver connectivity to the region. Many of Kenya's 50 million people are catered for by mobile coverage, but enormous sections of the country are outside the range of internet providers. Hence the benefits of one balloon to start with. What started life as a 'reserve big bet' for Google was 'destroyed' over five years into an 'adapt' option. From lots of balloons everywhere, down to one balloon in Kenya. Had Google started with this approach of one single balloon in any country in 2013, they would probably be much further along with Project Loon by now.

The strength of the Payoff Profiles Matrix lies in identifying the many ways to improve the payoff profile of your starting initiatives – and especially the unfortunate 'reserve big bets'. Over the years, I've commonly seen 20 to 30 per cent of any company's initiatives end up in that top right corner. So risky, and so unnecessary. Move them down, move them left or, better still, do both at once. Improving the payoff profile of initiatives is probably the most effective adjustment you can make to your future fortunes. It's a moment of creative problem solving, usually relying more on smarts, words, flair and project knowledge by the team than on big data or analytical prowess.

Discuss

The third big decision is to Discuss the 'shape big bets', in the top left corner of the grid. That's where the management team should really be spending its time: debating and staying well on top of the people delivering the initiatives. Why? Because this corner of the Matrix has the potential to massively affect the company's future, one way or the other. It represents the biggest reward harnessed to the biggest risk. The chips can fall one way or the other. A good team should invest a good chunk of time trying to check again if there isn't a smarter way to make these initiatives more 'options'-based rather than continuing with the current 'big bet' version.

Payoff Profiles and the Decisions

	SHAPE	ADAPT	RESERVE
BIG BETS	DISCUSS	? ←	DESTROY
OPTIONS		? ↙	? ↓
NO REGRETS		DELEGATE	

Drag

Now that you're familiar with moving initiatives around the Matrix, you can see that the best position on this grid (once we've delegated the 'no regret' moves) is the 'shape options' box. Any initiative fitting there will give you the positive rewards of the 'shape' dimension, and the lesser risks of the 'options' approach. So the fourth and final decision for you is to look at all your remaining initiatives, and Drag them to the 'shape options' box as much as possible. You'll be familiar by now with the specific initiative engineering required (less risk, more reward, revised process) to end up with a new version of the initiative whose Post-it position is closer to the desired payoff profile.

In summary

The optimal strategic outcome in a Payoff Profiles Matrix session is achieved by following a four-pronged approach to the 'moves'.

> **Delegate** all the **'no regret' moves**
> **Destroy** all the **reserve big bets**

> **Discuss** all the **shape big bets**, and
> **Drag** all other initiatives closer to the **shape options** box.

Payoff Profiles and the Decisions

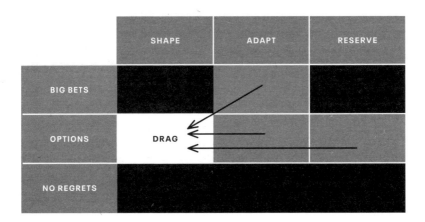

What we have here is effectively a twenty-first-century version of the BCG growth share matrix. The Payoff Profiles Matrix is a portfolio optimization tool that relies less on numbers and more on the intellectual agility of the participants. It demands of them the versatility to create slightly different versions of their starting initiatives, improving the payoff profile of each one in turn, and the overall company fortunes as a result.

Payoff Profiles example

The Payoff Profiles Matrix helps you optimize a company's strategic initiatives, whether these initiatives be external (new markets, new products, etc.) or internal (new processes, new technologies, etc.). For example, Unilever is following a strategy called Sustainable Living Plan, which contains many external and internal strands running in parallel.

On the external front, Unilever states on its website that it has '*a clear purpose – to make sustainable living commonplace – and a vision to grow our business while decoupling our environmental footprint from our growth and increasing our positive social impact'.*

This is built around three big goals.

> *Within 10 years: help more than a billion people to take action to improve their health and well-being (via hygiene, nutrition and other factors).*

> *Within 20 years: halve the environmental footprint of the making and use of Unilever products (in terms of greenhouse gases, water use, sustainable sourcing, waste and packaging), while still growing the business.*

> *Within 10 years: enhance the livelihoods of millions of people (via fairness in the workplace, opportunities for women, and inclusive business) while still growing the business.*

It's quite easy to imagine what a Payoff Profiles Matrix would look like that would capture all the initiatives being considered under each of the three big goals. For this example to make sense to you, however, you'd need quite a bit of specialist knowledge, in nutrition, greenhouse gases, industrial waste treatment, etc.

Let's talk instead about a Payoff Profiles Matrix applied to internal initiatives – which tend to be similar across most organizations, and thus easier to understand. For example, the '5Cs' framework that Unilever introduced to help its marketers adapt the grand strategic vision to their specific day-to-day activities. The 5Cs stand for Consumers, Connect, Content, Community and Commerce. In the words of Unilever's marketing boss, in 2017, to Emily Tan in *Campaign*:

> *Consumers: Keep the consumer as your 'true north'. The role of Unilever's brands is to help make life simpler by cutting through the chaos, anticipating the needs of the empowered consumer and providing assistance.*

> *Connect: While advertising isn't dying, it has to evolve. Today, it's about connecting in real time, in the context and with relevance. The digital ecosystem needs to be cleaned up or consumers will continue to get a poor experience online.*

> Content: Empowered consumers have better filters, and don't tolerate inauthenticity. 'People don't hate advertising, they hate bad advertising [. . .] We balance our assets across traditional interruption advertising and seek out content which specifically appeals to people's needs or passions.'

> Community: This is about 'harnessing the creative power of the 7 billion people on the planet'. Unilever will listen and engage with its community of consumers in real time, using data to co-create, build deeper relationships, and spot trends before they appear.

> Commerce: Is no longer just about buying. It's also about browsing, convenience, utility, experience and even entertainment. Unilever is experimenting with new business models, new ways to directly reach the empowered consumer.

Consumers, Connect, Content, Community and Commerce are not going out of fashion anytime soon, and this '5Cs' framework is relevant to most organizations today. It does represent, however, a big shift from established management practices. Imagine that the Learning and Development team at Unilever is therefore putting together a comprehensive list of projects and initiatives to help train the new leaders and managers. This includes guest speakers at lunchtime talks for hundreds of people, function-specific curated playlists on YouTube, micro budgets that individuals can spend on the skills building of their choice, etc. These various initiatives can be plotted on a Payoff Profiles Matrix like the one illustrated below.

The biggest component of the L&D team's budget is probably still the traditional Executive Education pot: sending 15 of the brightest minds in the global marketing function on a four-week residential course at Harvard or INSEAD. The L&D team is looking at ways to transform the payoff profile for this specific initiative. It's currently very much a 'reserve big bets': 'reserve' because every large corporation does it; 'big bet' because it's a big chunk of the L&D budget, and many people leave their sponsoring company when they return from the course.

In under an hour positioning the ideas in the Matrix, the L&D team could easily create a glide path to take the Executive Education item from the 'reserve big bets' corner all the way to the wonderful surroundings of a 'shape no regrets', in several moves.

Leadership Development at Unilever

The journey goes as follows, from the currently prevailing version A to the preferred future version F:

> **A:** Executive Education (month-long leadership development programme, in residential setting at prestigious school, such as Harvard, INSEAD)

> **B:** Shared Executive Education (same as A, but with additional participants invited from the company's current suppliers and partners)

> **C:** Development Sprint (week-long leadership development programme, delivered in-house rather than residential)

> **D:** Shared Development Sprint (week-long programme, delivered in-house, and with participants from suppliers' and partners' firms)

> **E:** Workshops (series of two-day leadership development sessions, delivered in-house, with examples and exercises on current issues, and with some guest participants)

> › **F:** Applied Future Workshops (same as E, but with guest
> participants from a larger circle of possible future suppliers
> and partner firms).

This example highlights four great benefits of the Payoff Profiles Matrix.

First and foremost, it is a simple and powerful way to help optimize individual ideas. Start with the version of an idea that the team has come up with, and then gradually engineer it towards less risk (travelling downwards in the Matrix) and more rewards (travelling leftwards in the Matrix), through verbal exchanges.

The second benefit of the Payoff Profiles Matrix is its Russian dolls quality. It can be deployed at the overall company level (for the three big external goals here). It can then be deployed for internal departmental initiatives (the 5Cs framework). And finally, it can be used at a functional level (the L&D team portfolio of training ideas).

The third benefit is the use of words rather than numbers. In most companies, many people are more comfortable with words than numbers, so more people can get involved in the Payoff Profiles Matrix. Likewise, generating ideas is usually done better in small teams, with three or four people riffing off one another's insights in a virtuous circle. Improving ideas, however, is usually done best with a larger crowd of 10 to 20 people, where everyone's expertise can be brought to bear on the removal of a small risk here, the addition of a small reward there, and so on.

The fourth benefit is resilience. Every few years – or months, in particularly fast-moving industries – you'll find that the exact position of any initiative in the Matrix will have shifted. Over time, initiatives that were once world-shaping have become more standard (i.e. 'adapt') if not expected (aka 'reserve'). This is a perfect opportunity to revisit all the initiatives, to shift them leftwards again in the Matrix.

This example illustrates how any company, like Unilever, can use the Payoff Profiles Matrix to plot and optimize its initiatives, at the corporate level and throughout the organization, in each business unit, department, function and team, at once and over time.

The Payoff Profiles Matrix in practice

The instructions below are for a typical session, usually with 10 to 20 initiatives and up to 20 people in the room. All you need for a good Payoff Profiles Matrix output are Post-its, marker pens and a wall or flipchart. You should also check out our app at www.strategic.how/payoff for a more memorable session.

> **Label the Initiatives** (5 mins)
> The object of a Payoff Profiles Matrix session is, first and foremost, to classify existing initiatives, so as to prioritize and improve the most valuable ones. This starts with a comprehensive list of the initiatives (the 'starting initiatives'). Use a catchy name for each initiative (typically between one and four words).

> **Plot the Initiatives** (10 mins)
> Draw a 3x3 grid. Label the rows from top to bottom as 'Big Bets', 'Options' and 'No Regrets'. Remind participants that this vertical dimension measures the level and nature of riskiness of any given initiative. Label the columns from left to right as 'Shape', 'Adapt' and 'Reserve'. Remind participants that this horizontal dimension measures the impact of that initiative on its environment – and therefore the likely reward for you, in due course. Plot the initiatives.

> **Take Stock and Adjust** (5 mins)
> Once all the initiatives have been plotted, you'll realize that a few of them 'feel in the wrong place' – there are always a few, and it is usually among the first initiatives plotted. The payoff profile for these initiatives doesn't appear to match the profile of the neighbouring initiatives in the grid. Adjust the position of these initiatives to better match the group consensus.

> **Optimize your Portfolio of Initiatives** (timing varies)
> Implement the following four decisions for all your initiatives, to end with a much improved risk–reward balance across your portfolio:

- **Delegate** all the 'no regret moves'
- **Destroy** all the 'reserve big bets'
- **Discuss** all the 'shape big bets', and
- **Drag** all the other initiatives closer to the 'shape options' box.

Payoff Profiles of the Initiatives

	SHAPE	ADAPT	RESERVE
BIG BETS			
OPTIONS			
NO REGRETS			

Here are four additional tips on how to use the Payoff Profiles Matrix in practice.

> **Tip 1:** When plotting the initiatives in the grid, do not spend more than 30 seconds on each one. Pick a first initiative, and ask each participant to vote 'big bet', 'options' or 'no regret' (to the tune of 'rock-paper-scissors') and by raising their hand high, medium or low. Ask them to vote on the horizontal axis using the same cadence for 'shape', 'adapt', 'reserve' and by pointing with their arm to the left, middle or right. Most voting generates a clear consensus, which saves time. Spend a bit longer debating the positioning on which there is no immediate non-verbal consensus.

> **Tip 2:** Don't explain too much the implication of the 'reserve big bets' box ahead of a Payoff Profiles Matrix session. Once participants know how bad this corner is, they'll usually avoid positioning too many initiatives in there – and you

might lose the value of getting to optimize these initiatives away from the corner (to the 'adapt' column, the 'options' row, or both). Better to acknowledge the bad starting position and to optimize it, rather than avoid seeing the problem in the first place.

> **Tip 3:** Use multiple colours of Post-its to chart the evolution in the payoff profile of the initiatives. Use one colour for 'starting initiatives', and another to show where the improved initiative finds itself positioned in the Matrix. A third colour might be useful for any additional improvements.

> **Tip 4:** Use the app at www.strategic.how/payoff. You can capture way more initiatives than with the wall-and-paper version. The latter tends to get really messy when there are more than 15 initiatives under consideration, and the app version has no such limits. Plus, you can more easily capture the evolving versions in the improvement of an initiative, and thus display the glide path that can take a 'reserve big bet' initiative all the way to the 'shape options' box.

Payoff Profiles exercise:
How to transform Facebook?

The Payoff Profiles Matrix is the first of three techniques we're seeing in our 'Down' journey, to help validate the ideas generated during an 'Up' session of strategic thinking.

With the Payoff Profiles Matrix, you give each of your initial ideas the opportunity to transform itself from a caterpillar (say, 'reserve big bet') into the most beautiful butterfly it can become (say, 'shape options', or even 'shape no regrets'). You then decide which combination of risk and reward works for you across your entire portfolio.

This approach is nearly the perfect complement to Mark Zuckerberg's historical recipe at Facebook of 'move fast and break things'. Here we might say 'move smart and think first'. Jumping ahead with the first version of your idea is nearly always a guaranteed recipe for a sub-optimal outcome.

Let's pretend that Mark Zuckerberg and Facebook are asking you to perform a Payoff Profiles Matrix exercise for the company today. Some of you might remember that on Thursday 26 July 2018, Facebook lost $120 billion in value . . . $120bn(!). Many factors combined to deliver this extraordinary blow, including falling rates of adoption, new data protection legislation in Europe (GDPR) and the increased prevalence of ad blockers. But the most important contributor was the announcement that several thousand humans would henceforth be recruited to work as content curators to police the site and users' newsfeed.

The latter is a classic instance of a 'reserve big bet'. It's a big bet, as it's both very expensive and very risky (there's a fair chance that it doesn't work in the long run). And it's a reserve move since, even in the best-case scenario, Facebook is just back to being a social network, still facing adoption, advertising and privacy issues.

Separately, Facebook is announcing every month some new initiatives to keep growing, including with Instagram and WhatsApp.

We therefore have two exercises for you to practise your Payoff Profiles Matrix skills now, and we invite you to share your solutions on www.strategic.how/payoff:

> **Payoff Profiles exercise #1:**
  plot your glide path for the Facebook initiative that is starting life in 'reserve big bet' as 'Recruit 3,000 human curators for the newsfeed'.

> **Payoff Profiles exercise #2:**
  plot, for all the latest newsworthy initiatives from Facebook you've heard of recently, your estimate of their starting position in the Matrix.

PAYOFF PROFILES EXERCISE #1:
GLIDE PATH FOR FACEBOOK'S HUMAN CURATORS INITIATIVE

NO REGRETS	OPTIONS	BIG BETS	
			SHAPE
			ADAPT
		Recruit 3,000 human curators for the newsfeed	RESERVE

PAYOFF PROFILES EXERCISE #2:
THE STARTING POSITION OF FACEBOOK'S LATEST INITIATIVES

	BIG BETS	OPTIONS	NO REGRETS
RESERVE			
ADAPT			
SHAPE			

6.

LANDSCAPE ANALYSIS

Five key data points

As we've just seen, spending an hour or so with the Payoff Profiles Matrix is a great way to initiate the 'Down' part of the Rollercoaster of Strategic Thinking. You start with the 10 to 20 ideas generated in the 'Up' part of the ride, and optimize your portfolio into 'no regret' moves, options and big bets. Usually, a few of these ideas will stand out, and they will then demand your further assessment and validation. Landscape Analysis is the process by which one gathers and uses data to help discriminate between these existing options.

How much data does one need to validate or invalidate an option? Two schools of thought and practice come into conflict here:

> the 'big data' school says: get as much data as possible.
> the 'sharp data' school says instead: get as little data as you need, as fast as you can.

I stand clearly with the latter school and would always rather have limited data, quickly, than a comprehensive dataset, way too late.

Too many people gather huge datasets, and interrogate them badly afterwards. The secret is to gather a very narrow dataset once you've identified the questions you want to ask. A good strategist should always be a bit lazy (i.e. refuse to manipulate data until it is strictly necessary). Keep thinking and thinking first, until you know exactly what data you want to manipulate, and what result you expect. Satisfaction comes from analysis that delivers the results you expect, and learning comes from analysis that delivers results you were not expecting! Satisfaction or learning are equally valuable outcomes; the faster the findings the better.

One truth of Landscape Analysis has stayed with me for years: 'On any strategic issue, there are only five key data points.' I heard this from the lips of a wise and wizened strategy consulting partner, and it struck a chord. I had been working in strategy consulting for nearly 10 years by then, and I too had started to notice that pattern. I had also started to sense a few more things, which he crystallized for me as follows.

'The most important aspect in any project is to identify quickly what those five data points are. Once you have this, you'll discover that two of these data points you already have; they were around you all along, you just didn't know they mattered. Two of the other data points you can gather through additional research (online surveys, face-to-face interviews, modelling, etc.). And the last data point will always remain elusive.

'Strategy is about the future and at least one aspect of the future will remain a mystery, no matter how hard you work at piercing the haze. One important implication of this is that you can never convince anyone of a new strategic idea through data alone – as you will always be one data point short of the perfect solution, or at least one data point short of the perfect proof for the solution you recommend. Once you accept that you'll always be one data point short of the perfectly convincing answer, your problem-solving life becomes simpler. It's all about speed.'

Remember, moving vertically to the Point of Clarity early in the project, and sharing initial options, gives your stakeholders the time to mull things over on their own too. When you come back and present your recommended solution at the end of the project, they will have had time to settle some of their anxieties around the various ideas and options. The data that you provide does not need to be as comprehensive as you might have feared, because your stakeholders bring their own thinking to the table.

On most projects today, the dataset you will start with is large enough to begin answering your question. You don't need to crawl along the Submarine path of Analytical Research, and collect additional dataset after dataset. Firstly because you probably have enough data to get started with the analysis, and secondly because you'll probably always be one or two critical data points short in the end. It's the hallmark of on-supply versus on-demand logic. The more things you have at hand, the more you find that what you want is not there. Let's turn to the world of entertainment (music, films, books, etc.) for an illustration of the different dynamics of on-demand and on-supply.

On-demand entertainment means you browse a *virtual* copy of the entertainment you want (a song, a book, a film, etc.) *before* you get it delivered to you. Some readers above the age of 30 will remember how on-supply entertainment meant you needed to accumulate a large *physical* inventory (of books, DVDs, CDs, vinyl, etc.) and you chose, *after* that, which one to consume on a given day. In on-supply, your choice is limited by what you have already accumulated to date; with on-demand your choice is endless on the right platforms. The world of entertainment shifted from entirely on-supply to nearly fully on-demand in the years after 2010.

The world of data shifted from on-supply to on-demand during the same period. Don't worry about first gathering all the data you can – because you will often be short of the perfect data you need, and because your thinking will be biased by the data you've accumulated to date. It's much better to focus on identifying the five key data points you need, work out the ones you already have, and then proceed to find the missing ones.

We'll see visual tools and examples of landscape analysis throughout this chapter. In order to keep them easy to absorb, we've intentionally selected industries that most readers will already be familiar with as consumers (clothes retail, insurance, toys, etc.).

Four key visual tools of Landscape Analysis

A useful way to identify where the five key data points might come from is through the four Quadrants of Landscape Analysis. In the validation of any new business idea there's always a demand side and a supply side, and you can look at each at both the macro level and the micro level.

Looking at the demand side at the macro level is usually called Market Analysis, and what one tackles there are issues of size, growth, market dynamics, segmentation, etc. The study of the demand side at the micro level is Customer Analysis, and it focuses more on key purchase criteria, satisfaction, loyalty, etc.

4 Quadrants of Landscape Analysis

	DEMAND	SUPPLY
MACRO	MARKET Analysis	INDUSTRY Analysis
MICRO	CUSTOMER Analysis	COMPANY Analysis

Assessing the supply side at the macro level is referred to as Industry Analysis, and it concerns itself with competitor profitability, industry concentration, economies of scale, etc. Finally, Company Analysis focuses on your own business, and in particular on issues of cost structure, margin levels, organizational structure, etc.

Each quadrant of landscape analysis comes with dozens of powerful tools and techniques – probably worthy of a whole book in their own right! In order to keep this chapter manageable, however, I've selected one key visual tool in each quadrant:

> **Mekkos** are the most versatile and comprehensive way to get to the heart of market analysis

> **GPS Chart** summarizes a vast amount of industry dynamics in one graph

> **Conversion Waterfall** helps visualize the essence of customer analysis, i.e. where do we satisfy customers and where do we lose them?

> **Line Profitability** is a never-failing insight into the possible mis-allocation of resources among the company's products or business units.

MEKKOS

Mekkos are probably the most powerful tools of Landscape Analysis. They're both a way to display market analysis information and, more broadly, a way to show three cuts at any dataset in one single chart. Let's have a look at one right away. Some of you have never seen a shape like this, and others will be a bit more familiar with it. When you're presenting a Mekko to an audience, you should always guide their eyes around the chart, so they understand what it is before you tell them what it shows. The Mekko name, by the way, comes from Marimekko, a Finnish design company, and any Mekko with lots of different colours looks like one of their very famous designs.

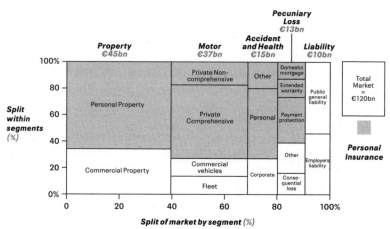

Mekko
(French Insurance Market, 2018)

What you have here is a picture of the French insurance market. The total size of the rectangle is the total size of the market. And then we see three cuts of the dataset. The first cut is horizontal. We cut this particular rectangle into five segments and the width of each segment is proportional to the size of the segments. For example, going from left to right, property insurance is about 40 per cent of the total French insurance market, motor insurance is another 30 per cent, accident and health is 10 per cent, etc.

The second cut of the data is vertical. In the property insurance segment, we can see that there are two sub-segments; with the commercial property sub-segment accounting for about 35 per cent of the segment, and personal property accounting for about 65 per cent. The same logic applies when we look at motor insurance, where we see the first sub-segment, fleet insurance, is 15 per cent of the segment; commercial vehicles insurance is another 15 per cent, etc. And then likewise in the other columns.

The third cut at the data is when you use colour to select things that go together. We've highlighted in grey here all the sub-segments of the insurance market that are about personal insurance.

We've spent about 20 seconds introducing the chart. Once your eyes have adjusted, you will recognize that a Mekko offers a very comprehensive map of whatever you want to look at, be it the French insurance market or anything else.

People use Mekkos for all sorts of things. You can display any data series in them, as long as the data within the series doesn't change sign. Either all the numbers are positive (sales, number of products, headcount, etc.) or all the numbers are negative (costs, etc.). The only data series you can't put in a Mekko are ones where the numbers change sign (profits, etc.). If you did a Mekko for the profits of various business units, some of them would be negative, and you wouldn't be able to show that very well.

A classic example of using a Mekko outside of market analysis is for headcount. The total rectangle would be the size of your workforce, and you can then split this by divisions, by grades within divisions, and maybe use the colours to identify growth. In another example, you can use a Mekko to represent the total costs of a company, displaying your cost structure in a way you've never seen before. The total rectangle is your total cost base, and the vertical and horizontal splits cut the total in two different ways.

In a nutshell, Mekkos are simple ways to present three cuts of the dataset in one place, usually in the context of market analysis. They are also versatile enough to be used in lots of different contexts. Mekkos are visually rich, and also a bit complicated to get into at first glance. Always guide the eyes of a new audience and they'll quickly get the benefit of the new map.

When validating a new business idea, always construct the three or four most useful Mekkos you can think of to help size up and visualize the challenges your idea is facing.

GPS CHART

Growth, Profitability and Size (GPS) are the holy trinity of business success. If you've got growth, and you're profitable and big, then life is really sweet. If you are a small business, unprofitable and not growing, then life is hard.

One of the things you try to do when looking at competitors is look for inspiration. You're trying to see which of your various competitors you could learn from. The GPS Chart helps put into perspective the different competitors with actual data, which helps you rise above the usual anecdotes and myths being bandied around in any industry.

For all the competitors you can find, plot their growth on the horizontal axis, and their profitability on the vertical axis. The third axis, the size of the bubbles, is used to plot their size (i.e. sales). To make the chart more visually striking, we set the axes to the average of the industry. The horizontal axis is raised upwards to cross the vertical axis at the average industry profitability. Likewise, the vertical axis is shifted towards the right to cross the horizontal axis at the average industry growth.

You then plot the competitors in your industry, and you see a couple of things. The first one is, not uncommonly, you'll find one of the biggest competitors right bang in the middle. Their sheer size affects both the weighted average profitability and the weighted average growth, and thus the dominant players in the industry are, unsurprisingly, often going to be in the middle of the graph. The second insight is that each quadrant in any GPS Chart points to very different competitor dynamics.

Let's look at the medical interim placement industry in the US: companies who offer doctors, nurses, etc. on an interim basis for hospitals. Company X is a smallish player in the industry and has managed to gather data on 11 competitors. They are now wondering which of these competitors to copy, or draw inspiration from.

GPS Chart
(US Medical Recruiters, 2017)

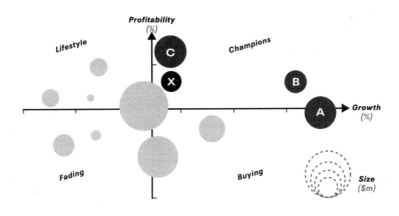

The bottom left quadrant contains companies that are fading; companies whose profitability is below industry average, and whose growth is below industry average. It doesn't matter what size they have, with below industry average growth and lesser profitability they're slowly fading away. The top left quadrant is the lifestyle corner, with companies that are not growing as fast as the industry, but are very profitable. They could compromise their high profitability if they really wanted to chase growth, but they would rather not, hence the lifestyle name.

The bottom right quadrant are the buying firms. They're growing a lot faster than the industry but at lower profitability. That's usually a giveaway for the fact that they're using discount pricing or other mechanisms to buy their growth. The top right quadrant is where the champions are. These are companies that achieve both above average profitability and above average growth, without compromising on either.

Company X is one such champion, and there are clearly three others in this industry: A, B and C. Company C is quite attractive because it's a lot more profitable than company X. So if X is interested in a bit of a lifestyle, they can find out how C does it, and adapt some of their recipes. Competitor A, on the other hand, is really going for growth, albeit with lower profitability. Company X is much better off looking at competitor B in greater detail. It's roughly the same size, with roughly the same profitability, but growing much faster than X. There is probably some really relevant learning to be derived from a further understanding of the actions of competitor B.

So in conclusion, a GPS Chart plots the holy trinity of business success in one chart (Growth, Profitability, Size) for as many competitors as you can find in one industry. Position the industry average in the middle of the graph, and you've got four quadrants to better understand the industry, and discover which are the best champions to draw inspiration from.

Building a GPS Chart can be quite fiddly, especially as the profitability data may not be easily available for many competitors (privately owned, divisions of large groups, etc.). It is, however, worth doing to avoid over-obsessing on irrelevant competitor anecdotes. If the Mekko presents a map of the battlefield of business (aka the market), then the GPS Chart offers a handy summary of the strategies of the various enemies on the field. Better make sure you draw inspiration from the competitors that are objectively successful, rather than being distracted by the ones you happen to have lots of anecdotal knowledge of (because of former employees having joined you, successful PR, etc.).

When validating a new business idea, always ask yourself whether this is something that the champions in your industry would do, or not, and assess the impact on profitability and growth.

CONVERSION WATERFALL

The Conversion Waterfall is a beautiful tool of customer analysis that helps you understand where you lose customers, and what to do about it. It posits that customers get converted from a standing start all the way to the purchase or usage of a product or service (however slowly or quickly that process happens), and that some of them get lost on the way. Think of a number of steps that customers typically go through, document the different ways in which the levels at the initial step become much lower at the final step, spot where you lose customers, and come up with remedial measures. Or assess your new ideas against the same drop in conversion.

Our example here comes from Uniqlo, the Japanese clothes retailer. Let's pretend that it is faced with a decision to alter its approach to market in Malaysia and the Philippines. In both countries, the proportion of the population that ever shop in Uniqlo stores (online and physical) is disappointingly low, at about 12 per cent. What are they to do about it? As it turns out, two ideas being contemplated by the organization are a big advertising campaign and a '3-for-2' in-store promotion. Both ideas do sound interesting and legitimate on paper, and need to be tested with numbers. (The same issue might affect Marks & Spencer in France and Spain, or Gap in Canada and Mexico, etc. Anywhere where a clothes retailer is faced with a difference in perception by customers in neighbouring markets.)

We could start by creating six steps on the horizontal axis, which answer the following questions in turn:

> **Awareness:** Are people aware of our brand?
> **Knowledge:** Do they know what we do?
> **Liking:** Are we one of their favourite suppliers?
> **Preference:** Do they prefer us?
> **Visit:** Do they visit often?
> **Purchase:** Do they purchase?

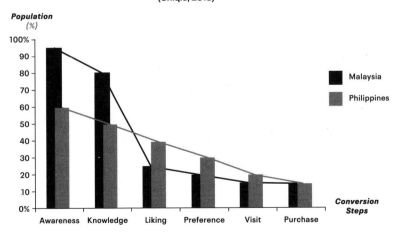

Conversion Waterfall
(Uniqlo, 2018)

Looking at the percentage of the populations who meet the various criteria, one can clearly spot two very different shapes. In Malaysia, great awareness, great knowledge, and then it dips at liking. But those who like Uniqlo convert really well into purchase. In the Philippines, by contrast, not as high a level of awareness to start with, but it trickles down all the way to the same level of purchase. Plotting in the Conversion Waterfall the actual data obtained from primary research (online surveys, face-to-face interviews, focus groups, etc.) helps diagnose the issues, and points to very different solutions, including a different assessment of the two ideas being considered.

In the Philippines, Uniqlo might decide to go ahead with the advertising campaign, which should increase awareness. The resulting higher level of awareness will hopefully trickle all the way down into higher sales, without too much 'leakage' along the way, through knowledge, liking, preference, etc. Additionally, the '3-for-2' in-store promotion should help convert the liking into preference, the preference into visit, and the visit into purchase.

In Malaysia, however, both ideas feel inappropriate. There's already a very high level of awareness and knowledge, so the advertising might be redundant. Likewise, the few people who do like Uniqlo do convert very well into purchase already, and so offering them a '3-for-2' in-store promotion would likely give away a lot of margin without adding much revenue. The company needs to rethink its initial ideas in light of the numbers. This is a classic illustration of the dive from Clarity to Certainty taking people away from Completion for a while. You think your ideas will be the solution, and then data shows that you need to think again. Not a huge problem, though, since the data gathered to complete the waterfall will help generate new ideas, and these will fare better at the waterfall test – since they will have been designed to do just that!

In summary, a Conversion Waterfall is a great way to diagnose the point at which you lose customers in a conversion process, which gives you a better understanding of why, and triggers thoughts on what you should do to improve your fortunes. **Where** leads to **why**, which leads to **what**.

When validating a new business idea, always construct the Conversion Waterfall to discover how the idea will help fix some of the existing 'leakage' your business faces, or if it doesn't help at all.

LINE PROFITABILITY

A lot of Company Analysis centres on discovering where your company actually makes money in practice. Line Profitability analysis is a beautiful way to understand the actual profitability of your business, at a very granular level (by product, by customer, etc.), even when the information is not immediately available.

We're going to refer to it throughout as XLP, where the X stands for whatever you want, and LP stands for line profitability – so you can have PLP (product line profitability), CLP (customer line profitability), SLP (supplier line profitability), etc. XLP means working out the profitability of your company by X (by product, customer, supplier, etc.) and taking better decisions as a result. A lot of companies still manage the allocation of their resources and decisions on the basis of gross margin, and you want to do so on a much more subtle level.

Below is the main chart outcome of a Product Line Profitability project I did a few years ago for the Toys R Us chain. Let's imagine these are the real numbers for three different products (Barbie dolls, giant fluffy pandas and batteries) which had roughly the same sales and the same growth.

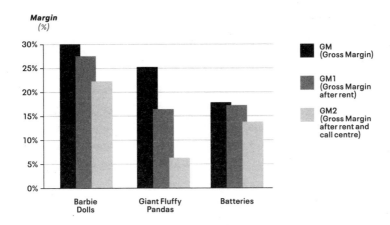

Line Profitability
(Toys R Us, 2013)

The graph clearly shows that Barbie dolls and pandas achieve a higher gross margin (GM). If that was the only profitability information available, your conclusion might well be to try and sell more Barbie dolls and pandas. As we've seen, however, the key to smart decisions here is to look below the gross margin level, at new levels of granularity that we'll call gross margin 1 (GM1) and gross margin 2 (GM2). In a retail environment like at Toys R Us these new margins may not be immediately available and have to be calculated. How do we do this? By looking at the remaining fixed costs at hand, and finding a way to allocate them smartly to each product category.

The biggest unallocated fixed costs are typically store costs – whether it's rent or depreciation. Those big costs exist because we put all these toys in the store itself, and so it's only fair that you check how much of the rent each product consumes. What is the driver of rent? It's square footage, and so we're going to allocate to each product a chunk of the rent, based on the square footage that this product occupies on the shop floor. After you go and measure the space that each of the products occupies, you might discover something that looks like GM1 in our graph.

Batteries occupy very little physical space, and are thus charged very little rent. As a result, the difference between GM and GM1 is minute for them. Dolls occupy a bit more space, and are charged a bit more rent in proportion. Giant fluffy pandas instead get charged a lot more of the rent, because they occupy a lot more of the space. Their margin after rent (GM1) is therefore much lower than for the other categories.

In any XLP analysis you then turn to the second biggest category of fixed costs to continue the discovery of actual cost consumption. In our example, let's pretend that this is the call centre. Any call centre is designed to handle all the customer requests or complaints for all the products, and that's a fixed cost. But arguably the reason there are five, 10 or 20 people on call is a function of the number of customer requests or complaints that are handled, which itself is a function of the product mix being sold. We just need to work out which products trigger these customer calls, and then charge back the relevant amount to each product.

We asked the call centre people what proportion of their time each category occupied. We discovered that dolls and batteries accounted for some of the requests, but that giant fluffy pandas were the leading cause of customer questions. ('How do I wash it?', 'My child has eaten some of the hair', etc.) So we allocated the call centre costs to each product category in proportion to the number and length of call centre interactions they consumed. Examining the outcome at GM2 in the graph, it is clear that pandas are a lot less profitable than they appear at first glance. Sure, they have a nice gross margin, but they then consume a lot more of the company's other costs (rent, call centres, etc.) in an invisible fashion. It is worth finding alternative strategies for giant fluffy pandas (occupy less display space, launch smaller versions, add washing instructions, etc.), if not alternative products altogether (more batteries, more compact fluffy products, etc.).

In summary, XLP is a process. Take some products (or customers, or suppliers, etc.), look at their gross margin, find the next set of unallocated costs, and allocate them to each category in proportion to the actual amount of these costs that the category consumes. You've got to decide on an allocation key (by square foot for rent, by minutes of interactions for call centres, etc.) and you might try a few before getting it right. The outcome will help you take better, more subtle business decisions.

When validating a new business idea, always think through the many Line Profitability angles (XLPs). You may not want to carry out a full analysis on every idea, but working out the 'hidden consumption' will give you a better feel for the likely true impact.

IN SUMMARY

We've seen four visual tools that help you discriminate between the various options generated in the 'Up' phase of any strategic rollercoaster exercise. Some are quite data heavy (GPS, XLP) others are lighter (Mekko, Waterfall). They are worth populating with real numbers, if you have the time and budget to do so. Failing that, just thinking through these tools will give you new insights and help you rate your initial ideas differently.

Landscape Analysis example

Let's now turn to a long example, where the critical data needed is very specific, and different from the four tools we've seen so far. Imagine a retail chain, with stores all across the UK, that is looking to reduce its store staff costs by 10 to 15 per cent. An 'Up' effort has already identified 10 to 20 ideas to help achieve that. Among them: cut salaries, reduce overtime, fire store managers, move employees to zero hours contracts, add self-service tills, rebalance store formats, incentivize full-time staff, train part-time staff, etc. The chain is made up of 400 stores, with 10 employees per store on average, and one designated manager per store.

Let's take the time to look in detail at one of the ideas: firing store managers. What are the five data points critical to validating whether this idea would work or not?

Before we go into that in detail below, I suggest you find a piece of paper and a pencil, and have a go at it on your own first. Reread the previous two paragraphs above to start with some limited background data, then take a few minutes to identify the critical data points you would want to address, before continuing.

The first critical data point for validating the idea of firing store managers is the managers' employment costs as a percentage of total store staff costs. If managers collectively don't account for at least 10 per cent of the total staff costs, then even firing all of them won't deliver the sought-after savings. Any retail chain would have that information at its fingertips. In our case, the finance department informed us within 24 hours that store managers did account for 23.6 per cent of total store staff costs.

The second critical data point for validating the idea is the proportion of stores geographically near enough to one another to make it feasible for a store manager to cover two stores. Indeed, with the current practice of one manager per store, the moment we fire the only manager in one store we would implicitly move the staffing model in one of two logical directions: no manager per store at all, or one manager for every two stores.

In the first scenario, if this initial store can survive without any manager, why wouldn't all stores survive without managers? In this instance, the percentage of stores without managers would become 100 per cent. In the other legitimate scenario, once a store manager has been fired, then the manager from the nearest store spreads his or her responsibility to cover the newly manager-less store. If this approach can work for this pair of stores, then it could work for any other pair of stores, and the number of managers can, in theory, be cut by 50 per cent. In practice, there would be stores too far from their nearest neighbour, say on Scottish islands or Welsh mountains, and therefore the maximum percentage will be somewhat shy of 50 per cent. How far below 50 per cent is critical to the success of the initiative? Luckily, all retail chains know the exact location of their stores, and the property department informed us, in this case, that 360 stores (or 90 per cent of the 400 total) had another store within 30 minutes' drive.

This means that the chain could keep all the managers in the 40 isolated stores, fire 45 per cent of managers, and ask the remaining 45 per cent of managers to cover two stores each. The total savings in this instance would amount to 10.6 per cent of total store staff costs (= 23.6% x 45%), which is in the ballpark of what we need to keep the idea alive (i.e. above 10 per cent savings in store staff costs). The scenario that would fire all store managers would, of course, mean cost savings of 23.6 per cent, in theory, but it would also be wildly riskier, and is shelved for now.

A third critical data point to validate our idea would be the views of the store managers themselves. They will be the ones directly in charge of implementing the new approach. Clearly, some data on their take on this matters immensely. There are four main dimensions to gathering these store managers' views: how many of them do we talk to, who specifically do we choose to talk to, how many questions do we ask them, and what questions exactly?

Two schools of thought and practice come into conflict here again. The 'big data' school says: ask as many questions of as many people as possible. The 'sharp data' school says instead: ask as few questions as possible, of as few people as possible, but do it as fast as possible. I'm very much with the latter school: give me a bit of data really quickly, rather than a lot of data later. I want to start testing things right away – and we can always ask for more data later, if need be.

In our case here, we had 24 hours to come back to the management team. We felt the views of 10 store managers would be enough, that early in the validation process, to nudge the day one way or the other. Managers being busy people, some would not answer within the 24 hours, so we needed to plan for 20 conversations.

What do we ask them? The classic 'big data' approach is 'everything we can think of'. My preferred 'sharp data' approach suggests undertaking a multi-stage refining exercise, to end up asking one question, and one question alone, but making it as critical as possible. Our first version of that question was: 'Would you like to run two stores?' This version, however, introduces a distorting filter between what we want and what we'll get, which is the respondents' appetite for career progression. We refined the sentence into: 'Could you run two stores?' This version removes the career filter, although it introduces another filter, self-awareness. Some respondents might reply that they could run two stores when they actually couldn't, while others who could do it might reply negatively. In order to remove this cognitive bias, our third version was more objective with: 'What would one need to do to run two stores?' This phrasing effectively removes the filters of ambition and self-awareness. The slight drawback might be the length of the answers we'd be getting from respondents. Our final version, designed to keep answers short while completely on point, became: 'What would prevent you from managing two stores?'

It takes a while to sharpen the initial version of the question into the best possible question one ends up with. In our example here, imagine for a second what the spreadsheets with the answers would look like under the four successive versions. It then becomes clear that the time spent crafting a sharper question is well invested. The compilation of the answers of 10 store managers to the last version of our question will go a long way towards reassuring the senior management team of the validity of the idea. If the list of these conditions can be met by the management team, while still exceeding the target economic benefits, then the idea is still worth testing and validating further.

There is one final question to address: who do we ask? Clearly, we want the store managers whose views are the most predictive of the future. We don't need to hear from managers whose store is isolated, nor from managers who would be made redundant (likely found in the bottom half of the store managers' performance table). We want to hear from some of the 45 per cent of managers who would end up being kept, and asked to run two stores. Let's focus on the ones within that group who would find this the hardest – typically people just above the average, rather than the stars – and let's ask them.

The few minutes we did spend identifying the preferred character-istics of respondents gave us a double benefit: it made it easier for HR to give us a list of which specific 20 store managers to call, and it made the results of the survey much more convincing for the management team at the end. The store managers we didn't interview were the ones who were more likely to find the idea easier to implement. The sample of people we did interview was therefore a worst-case scenario, and all the more convincing than a random selection of store managers – including any much larger, but less focused, selection. 'Sharp data' always trumps 'big data'.

A fourth critical point that would help quickly convince stakehold-ers of the validity of our idea would be some relevant competitor anecdotes. We don't need a full-blown benchmark, with dozens of com-petitors, etc. Finding one or two sufficiently relevant companies that are already operating under something like the new model we have in mind should be enough to assuage the management team's doubts.

How do you get to this data? One huge resource for the 'sharp data' people is Google, of course. Type in the search box exactly what you want ('one manager for two stores' in this case) and pray that the results pages give you exactly what you hope for!

The fifth critical data point here is the extent to which the shift to one manager across two stores will impact customer satisfaction, staff work ethic, etc. – and, more broadly, the results of the stores. There is no point trying to save costs now by firing 45 per cent of the managers, if this leads to worse performance in the market a few months later, in an unintended but somewhat likely consequence. This fifth data point would be wonderfully useful, but it will remain elusive until the chain has a go at testing the idea with actions in practice. As previously noted, this is a classic example of being one data point short of the perfectly convincing solution.

To recap, the five key data points to help validate the idea of firing store managers as a way to reduce store staff costs by 10 to 15 per cent turned out to be:

> **A:** managers' actual employment costs as a percentage of total staff costs
> **B:** percentage of stores near enough another store (say 30 minutes' drive)
> **C:** existence of competitor(s) already doing 'one manager for two stores'
> **D:** sample of relevant managers' views on the initiative, and
> **E:** net impact of the initiative on store results in a few months' time.

If we map these data points on the four Quadrants of Landscape Analysis, we can see that we've got the supply side covered, but we're a bit thin on the demand side.

Example of Landscape Analysis

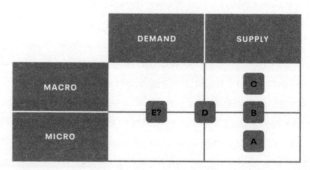

There are two ways to remedy that: interview customers, or test the idea on them. Find out what they have to say about the idea, or find out what they would actually do about it. In this example, as in many business instances, actions speak louder than words, and we will see in the following 'Lean Startup' chapter that it's time to small-scale test the idea.

In the meantime, let's have a go at fixing Starbucks New Zealand.

Landscape Analysis exercise: How to fix Starbucks New Zealand?

Every instance of Landscape Analysis is its own unique little world. Sometimes data exists before ideas have been generated, and other times the ideas are there and need to be validated. Usually, a mixture of the two approaches prevails.

Imagine that you are an internal consultant at Starbucks' head office in Seattle, and you've just been asked to improve the performance of the 10 Starbucks stores in New Zealand. These stores are all located in various office areas of Auckland, the biggest city in the country. They serve the local working population with breakfast and lunchtime food and drinks. The main product groups are: coffee, sandwiches, cakes, cold drinks, and other. Our example could equally cover 10 Costa Coffee stores in Doha, Qatar, or 10 Caffè Nero stores in Warsaw, Poland. The key question for the project is simply, 'How can we improve profits in our existing 10 stores?'

The team has already put together a series of possible ideas that include the following:

A. get rid of cakes
B. prepare sandwiches off-site
C. offer cake discounts with every coffee
D. train baristas to make coffee faster, and
E. close stores 4 and 9.

A junior member of the team has already started compiling data, including a quick interview with the general manager of Starbucks New Zealand, a weekly income statement, weekly store sales by product, and weekly wastage by product.

You can find an Excel file with all the data on www.strategic.how/ landscape, and we invite you to share your solutions to the two exercises of Landscape Analysis:

> **Landscape Analysis exercise #1:**
> what initial view (yes, maybe, no) would you take in the case
> of the five ideas listed above so far (a, b, c, d, e), based on
> your analysis of the available data?

> **Landscape Analysis exercise #2**

are stores 4 and 9 performing badly because they carry so many sandwiches, or are they bad regardless (please offer specific analysis to support your answer)?

The best analysis to help you answer these questions are two Mek-kos (products by store, and stores by product) and two Line Profitability slides (by product, and by store).

The Store Line Profitability work is best carried out after the Product Line Profitability analysis, and both XLPs should have GM1 as gross margin after wastage, and GM2 as gross margin after wastage and labour.

LANDSCAPE ANALYSIS EXERCISES #1 AND #2: GENERAL MANAGER INTERVIEW

'I think all our stores are at their maximum potential sales, but I think some stores are probably slack on costs. In terms of labour cost, when stores are working efficiently, coffee and sandwiches should use twice as much labour per pound of sales as the other product categories. I think that store 4 should be able to live with around NZ$500 per week of waste without hurting sales, and store 9 around NZ$300 a week. I think that both these stores should be able to operate with labour levels no more than 33 per cent higher as a percentage of sales than the other stores.'

Weekly income statement (NZ$)

Sales		**63,000**
COGS		**29,690**
Coffee	13,760	
Sandwiches	9,150	
Cakes	3,055	
Cold drinks	2,535	
Other	1,190	
		GM
Wastage		**5,380**
		GM1
Store Costs		**20,100**
Labour cost	12,000	
Rent	3,100	**GM2**
Rates	1,000	
Heat and power	1,000	
Telephone	500	
Repairs and renewals	500	
Cleaning materials	350	
Printing and stationery	250	
Bank commission	200	
Insurance	200	
Sundries	1,000	
Head Office Costs		**4,000**
Profit		**3,830**

Weekly sales (by product)

$/week	Coffee	Sandwiches	Cakes	Cold drinks	Other	TOTAL
Store 1	5,700	3,700	1,200	1,200	200	12,000
Store 2	6,500	2,000	500	500	500	10,000
Store 3	5,500	1,500	600	300	100	8,000
Store 4	1,500	3,500	500	400	100	6,000
Store 5	3,000	2,000	400	300	300	6,000
Store 6	2,700	1,500	500	150	150	5,000
Store 7	3,800	600	100	400	100	5,000
Store 8	3,300	1,000	300	300	100	5,000
Store 9	500	2,000	300	150	50	3,000
Store 10	1,900	500	300	200	100	3,000
TOTAL	34,400	18,300	4,700	3,900	1,700	63,000

Weekly wastage (by product)

$/week	Coffee	Sandwiches	Cakes	Cold drinks	Other	TOTAL
Store 1	171	481	228	12	20	912
Store 2	195	240	105	5	65	610
Store 3	165	195	126	3	9	498
Store 4	60	1,050	150	4	12	1,276
Store 5	90	240	88	–	30	448
Store 6	81	195	105	3	5	389
Store 7	114	72	17	–	2	205
Store 8	66	120	63	3	3	255
Store 9	20	560	60	–	1	641
Store 10	38	47	58	–	3	146
TOTAL	1,000	3,200	1,000	30	150	5,380

7.

LEAN STARTUP

Lean Startup in action

So far we've seen two ways to eliminate options in no time: with words (Payoff Profiles Matrix) or with numbers (Landscape Analysis). A third way to eliminate options quickly is with actions. Particularly with quick, cheap and information-rich actions; whether you call them experiments, tests, prototypes, etc. Sometimes a simple action is worth a hundred words, or a thousand numbers, in helping you check if an option is likely to work out.

Of all the initiatives that a business can undertake, IT projects have had notoriously very bad success rates down the years; often coming in late and over budget, when not downright failing. A whole school of thought started in the 1990s in California to try and remedy this terrible success rate – and it resulted in the Lean approach, sometimes also referred to as the Agile method.

The Lean or Agile approach posits that an organization is just a portfolio of tests, and that customers hold the key to its future. As a result, the best strategy for any new company, or new venture, is to discover its optimal path to success through frequent interactions between customers and any new thing being developed.

Prominent among the thinkers of the Lean school are Steve Blank and Eric Ries. I definitely recommend Eric Ries' book *The Lean Startup: How Constant Innovation Creates Radically Successful Businesses* and Steve Blank's *Harvard Business Review* article 'Why the Lean Startup Changes Everything'.

According to both, the most important guarantee for long-term success is early and quick experimentation. Success comes to the companies that are best and fastest at validating their ideas quickly, and correcting course accordingly. You might have heard the mantra 'Fail fast, fail often, fail forward'. In plain English: test with actions as soon as you can, test as many ideas as you can, and learn from your failed tests.

Most businesses hesitate to test ideas through actions. For two main reasons. First, they wait too long before testing an idea, and so can't fail fast. Second, they do not design experiments that are small enough, and thus can't afford to fail often.

To circumvent these issues, Eric Ries and the Lean school invite us to change our approach to testing our business ideas. They recommend that we work in short, incremental and iterative product development cycles, rather than in a linear way off a pre-determined workplan. Replace the old triumvirate of 'plan, decide, launch' with the more flexible 'test, learn, roll-out', and cycle between test and learn quite a few times, in a feedback loop.

The Lean Startup feedback loop starts with an idea. For each idea, you quickly build a simple version of your product, measure customer actions, and learn from the data generated, to help you improve the idea. And on and on, through the feedback loop.

Ries' Lean Startup

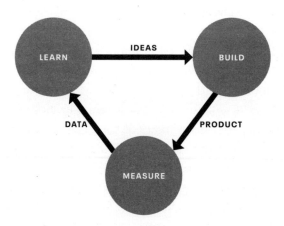

The Lean Startup feedback loop (or Build–Measure–Learn loop) emphasizes speed as a critical ingredient of options validation. A team or company's effectiveness is determined by its ability to cycle quickly several times through the feedback loop. A specific idea's viability is determined by its ability to survive quite a few such cycles. There are five key aspects to consider when setting up the loop.

MINIMUM VIABLE PRODUCT (MVP)

An MVP is the version of a new product which allows a team to collect the maximum amount of validated learning about customers, with the least effort. The goal of an MVP is to test the fundamental hypotheses contained in any new idea, and to begin the learning process as quickly as possible.

For example, opening a new restaurant contains at least four hypotheses: that enough customers will like the food, that the chef will regularly deliver the same quality of food at scale, that enough customers will come to the chosen location, and that the venture will be profitable. These four hypotheses (appeal, production, location, economics) are best tested separately, and successively, with different MVPs, rather than all at once, together.

The first MVP might well be as simple as cooking at home for a few friends, to test the appeal of the intended food. Once that is successful, a second MVP could take the shape of a food truck. This would help test the appeal further, and validate the ability to produce quality predictably. A third MVP in the shape of a fixed pop-up store would further test appeal and production, together with location and economics.

ACTIONABLE METRICS

Actionable metrics are those that lead to informed business decisions and subsequent actions. In contrast, 'vanity metrics' are those that do not accurately reflect the key drivers of a business.

For example, page views are actionable metrics for the *Guardian* (with a business model still reliant on advertising), and vanity ones for *Bloomberg* (with its entirely subscription-based business model). Whenever you run a Lean Startup test, it is essential to identify beforehand the metrics you seek to optimize, and what success would look like.

A/B SPLIT TESTING

This is an experiment in which different versions of a product, service or experience are offered to two different customer groups at the same time. The goal is to observe changes in behaviour between the two groups and to measure the impact of each version on an actionable metric.

For example, many video streaming companies (Netflix, Prime Video, Disney+, etc.) are permanently improving the way they display content to their users through A/B split tests, showing different users different content curation solutions. The actionable metrics might be the number of new show thumbnails a viewer will click on, as well as the number of episodes of each show a viewer will subsequently watch. A succession of A/B split tests help reveal the approach to content curation that best drives the actionable metrics.

Please note that in a pre-Lean mode, the decision regarding which content curation approach to take might have been left to furious debates between senior editors and curators, fighting for their own choice on the back of personal experience, personal taste and political influence. Not always the best guarantee for the optimal solution.

CONTINUOUS DEPLOYMENT

The process whereby anything pertinent to the business is immediately deployed into production. For digital businesses, it can be deploying code as often as 50 times a day.

In the example above, streaming and video-on-demand sites commonly deploy new solutions on a daily basis. Physical businesses typically experience slower roll-out rates, but many retailers still spread newly tested successful practices across their estate on a weekly or monthly basis.

PIVOT

A structured course correction designed to test a new fundamental hypothesis about the product, strategy and engine of growth. Any experiment will usually test several assumptions at once. A failed experiment might be down to only one failed assumption. If the other assumptions turned out positive, then maybe there is value to be delivered and captured through these alone?

For example, Groupon started life as a social activism entity. It tried and tested two assumptions: 1) it could gather large groups at short notice in the physical world around a common cause, and 2) the individuals gathered that way could achieve a quick social impact for their cause of choice. When assumption 2 was proved wrong, but assumption 1 passed the test, Groupon still had something of value, and they pivoted to the collective discount website we know today.

IN SUMMARY

In order to test quickly the validity of any of its new ideas, a company needs to build a Minimum Viable Product (MVP), identify actionable metrics, measure results with real customers, and learn from that experiment. In other words, the Lean Startup approach to testing an idea with actions is a learning cycle. It turns this idea into built products, measures customers' reactions and behaviours against these products, and then decides whether to persevere or pivot the idea; and this process repeats as many times as necessary.

Testing with Lean

The Lean or Agile approach to quickly testing ideas is very powerful. Its most famous embodiment, the Lean Startup, began life helping small digital ventures find their place in ill-defined fields. Over time, the principles contained in the Lean approach have spread to all corners of the business world.

Big digital companies (Google, Amazon, Facebook, etc.) have embraced the Lean approach. All of them are permanently trying out new service lines, typically in faraway countries. If the new service works, it is then 'rolled out' across the whole company. 'Rolling out' is to the Lean approach what 'big launch' was to linear work-planning. It is easy to see how Lean practitioners can also be called Agile. 'Test, learn, roll-out' is so much more flexible than 'plan, decide, launch'.

Lean Startup Applicability

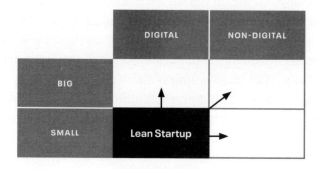

Small non-digital companies are also on board with the Lean Startup approach. For example, we've seen earlier that nobody in their right mind opens a restaurant from scratch any more. Every aspiring restaurateur goes through three or four feedback loops of MVPs and measurement before committing real money to a venture. The classic successive MVPs might be cook for friends first, offer catering next, then rent a food truck, negotiate a pop-up, and finally open a fully fledged restaurant. Each successive MVP is only embarked upon if and when the results from the previous tests have turned out positive.

Finally, many big, non-digital companies have migrated to a Lean approach too. Whether they label it Agile, Sprint, Scrum, Lean, etc. Many labels, one shared principle: nothing gets launched at scale without some significant element of customer validation first. And that means getting real customers to do things in order to validate the critical hypotheses underlying your new idea. General Electric has a joint-venture with Eric Ries, whereby any big project at GE gets examined in detail, and put on a Lean path to success, with MVPs, experiments and a feedback loop.

Working with large digital and non-digital clients over the years, I would like to add three rules of my own that are essential in my experience, even if rarely mentioned in the Lean literature. These are my three additional rules for the application of Lean by established entities.

TEST YOUR CRITICAL HYPOTHESES ON PAPER FIRST, AND AGAIN AND AGAIN

It's easy to test anything and everything. What are the hypotheses that are critical to the test's success (i.e. those where failure would kill the idea altogether)? Design the MVP to ruthlessly focus on them, at the expense of any other 'nice to have' data.

There is only so much failure that humans and established organizations can take. Every failure takes its toll. Sometimes organizations have translated the Lean approach of 'test and learn' into 'test to learn'. I strongly push back against that. One of the most common lessons that people learn from a failed test is that they don't like the taste of being proved wrong! Failure is a strong medicine. What doesn't kill you makes you stronger indeed. But who wants to live on a diet of cough medicine? Tests should be used sporadically, when the outcome is genuinely unknown, and the difference between outcomes is meaningful.

Otherwise, it's just a poll. There's a big difference between a test and a poll. A poll is not knowing which shade of blue to go with for your logo, and showing five versions to 10,000 people and finding out which is the most popular. A test is having the hypothesis that a darker shade of blue will appear more serious and reliable, which will lead to more purchases (for example) and validating this against another lighter shade of blue.

CREATE THE MVP WITH BORROW, BARTER AND BEG, RATHER THAN BUY OR BUILD

Any MVP that we use for a test will cease to have any value after the test. Either the test fails, and the idea is then abandoned (together with the MVP), or the test succeeds, and the idea is tested further through a newer MVP. In both instances, the elements assembled together for that initial MVP are probably destined for the scrap heap.

Which is why any MVP should not be bought or built, but instead should be borrowed, bartered or begged for. Can we call in a favour from a third party (a supplier, a distributor, a friend, etc.) to get access to some external resources for very little time or cash, maybe in exchange for internal resources? Only spend real cash as a very last resort.

A codicil of this is that variable costs trump fixed costs. One of the key rules of business is always to seek a lower unit cost, typically through costs that are more fixed than variable. We actually try and achieve the exact opposite here, during a Lean experiment. The more variable the cost, the more we only pay for data.

INVEST IN HIDE-ABILITY AND DENIABILITY

Most tests fail. Let's make sure the failure doesn't have a negative impact on our brand or reputation. Not only should the scale of the first test be small, but its failure should not have any negative impact beyond the sadness of seeing one's great hopes crushed.

Young startups often believe that bad publicity is better than no publicity. Established companies don't have this luxury. Bad publicity must be avoided at all costs. Most people would also prefer not to be tarred forever with an idea or a venture that didn't work out.

Two of the most classic ways to build hide-able and deniable MVPs are to test in out-of-the-way locations, and to involve another company with very different risk exposure. Starting your MVP in a sparsely populated part of a country that isn't your home market will ensure that you minimize coverage of any mishaps. Likewise, asking yourself 'Which company couldn't care less if our worst-case scenario materialized?' is a great way to identify who you want to partner with on the test.

As a final word of caution, the Lean/Agile approach is not the answer to everything. Like all techniques in the 'Down' part of the Rollercoaster of Strategic Thinking, the Lean technique is dependent upon your starting conditions. If your initial ideas are terrible, no matter how much Lean testing you put them through, you'll still end up with the best of a bad bunch. The best way to ensure a successful outcome is often to redo a session of 'Up' idea generation after a failed Lean Startup test.

Lean testing example

In the 'Happy Line' chapter, we discussed possible ways for a train operator to better satisfy its customers. Whether that operator was Avanti in the UK, Amtrak in the US, NSW TrainLink in Australia, etc. One of the resulting ideas was a standing-room-only carriage. This was felt to offer potentially a better trade-off of benefits for some customers: less comfort, but for a much cheaper price.

How does one find out quickly if this idea has legs, or is destined to fail? So far we've seen three ways to qualify this idea: with words (Payoff Profiles), with numbers (Landscape Analysis) and with actions (Lean Startup). Some of you might already be thinking of ways to test the standing-room-only carriage with words and numbers, but let's focus on actions here.

In order to offer a realistic illustration of the Lean method in practice, I'd like to spend a tad longer going through the many questions and answers that take place in the minds of the test organizers as they work out the exact size and shape of the experiments they are about to conduct, and the hypotheses they seek to test.

QUESTIONS AND ANSWERS

What is the critical hypothesis?

Is it whether people can stand in trains? No, that happens already, when trains are full. Is it whether people would willingly stand in trains? No, that happens already, when passengers choose to go and stand in the bar carriage for a drink. Is it about how long people would willingly stand in trains on average? Yes. That average duration is the key measurement we're going to seek to get from our experimentation with an MVP.

Our critical hypothesis is therefore best expressed as: 1) enough people will, 2) willingly stand in trains, 3) for long enough, 4) meeting safety rules, 5) to economically justify a standing-room-only carriage on many of our trains.

How can we increase the likelihood of passing the test?

The average duration is the core aspect of our hypothesis, and there are four ways to increase it during the test:

> build a smoother train ride (train tracks, carriage suspension, etc.)
> muscle-up passengers (better posture, stamina exercises, etc.)
> distract passengers (people to talk to, entertainment to watch, etc.)
> incentivize passengers (discounted tickets, additional train miles, etc.).

You will recognize from the 'Pyramid Principle' chapter that the four options above add up to a level in a Pyramid. If all four options work out, then the outcome is clearly a good idea, but not all four conditions need to be true for the outcome to be a good idea. The Lean Startup approach recommends testing ideas with a Minimum Viable Product, and my own tips suggest you beg, borrow, barter rather than buy or build. In practice, at this stage, let's create a test carriage, with distractions and incentives. Muscling-up the passengers might be too cumbersome, and building a smoother train ride is definitely too time consuming and too expensive at this point.

What distractions should we use?

As always in experiments and tests, make sure you don't have too many variables being tested at once. In this case, where do people already willingly stand for long stretches of time? In bars, at music gigs, and at some sporting events. Let's therefore bring a minimalist version of all three to our test carriage. A bar, a couple of screens with sporting events, and a stage at the back with a live musician (covering a range of music genres with broad appeal).

How do we put together this carriage?

A first idea might be to borrow a bar carriage from a supplier before it goes into service. Another one might be to turn to our own maintenance team, and ask to borrow a 'naked' carriage straight out of maintenance. Set up a temporary bar, stage and screens (meeting health and safety standards) and you're ready to roll. I call that the supply-side element. You could also call it the Minimum Viable Product.

The other aspect of a Lean experiment is the demand side. We need to carefully work out which customers we want to share our MVP with, how we're going to invite them to take part in the test, and what are the risks involved in the test.

Who should our target customers be for this test?

Anyone who values a cheaper ticket in exchange for a possibly more social and more entertaining, but physically more demanding travel experience. While anyone could meet the profile, it is clear that students and young adults, in general, fit it particularly well. Let's first try and get them to take part.

What are the risks involved in our test?

Firstly stamina: people might get physically or mentally tired of standing for too long. We could mitigate that by allowing them to go back to a seating carriage if they wish. A second risk would be the rowdiness, and associated consequences of too many people drinking and standing in a vehicle moving at speed (vomiting, urinating, fighting, etc.). We could mitigate that by having non-alcoholic drinks only, at least to start with. The final risk is, as often, a reputation risk, if the test is aborted (for whatever reason) and a journalist decides to report our failure in unsympathetic terms. We'll see shortly how to mitigate that risk.

Where should we run the test?

(NB: While minimizing the risks of unwitting exposure.) Let's carefully choose the test train line. We are probably looking at a line with a high proportion of young adults and students, with a far enough end destination to test stamina, and slightly out of the way of the national media – to avoid negative coverage before the test is either terminated or ready for prime-time exposure. In Britain, for Avanti, these conditions probably point to a train line like Birmingham to Bangor.

How should we invite our target customers to take part?

(NB: While minimizing the risks of unwitting exposure.) There are four main options for making our target customers aware of the new carriage:

> on our website
> in the ticket offices of the stations on the route
> on the platforms of the stations on the route, and
> on board the trains.

The website and the ticket offices might be a tad too broad (in that they'll alert lots of unintended targets too), and on board the trains might be a bit too late (people might be unwilling to try out the standing-room-only carriage once they've already sat down, stored away their belongings, etc.). The optimal choice is probably a physical presence on the relevant platforms on the route.

A couple of Avanti employees might be standing next to a great big banner that would read: 'FREE TRAIN TRAVEL TODAY. Ask us and we'll reimburse your ticket.' Please note that the actual text of the banner could be A/B split tested until the most successful wording is arrived at.

Once passengers approach the Avanti agents they could be told that they can travel for £1, provided they stand the whole way, in the new, richly appointed 'Fun carriage' (containing a bar, sports on TV screens, musicians on a stage, etc.). The percentage of passengers who take up the agents on their offer will be a pretty good indication of the likely popularity of the new business idea. We can surmise that a few things might adjust that percentage over time:

> advertising: the more people know about the offer, the more people prepare for it, and take it up when presented with it at the station

> convenience: we would make the option to book for the carriage conveniently available on the website itself, which will likely increase attendance

> habit: some people might grow into the 'Fun carriage', while others might hate it and not visit it again – whatever improvements we make to it

> pricing: varying the price of the tickets would test the exact trade-off between sitting and comfort that passengers prefer

> alcoholic drinks: adding alcoholic drinks in due course has to be part of the test, to mimic likely real-life conditions.

All these aspects suggest that we will be able to significantly influence the ongoing percentage of users, if and when the service is fully up and running. Not all of the influencing factors will be possible economically, though. Hence testing a 'base case' with our MVP. Extreme customer responses (be it zero interest or massive over-subscription) are very conclusive, and can send us straight to a conclusion. More often than not, the first MVP helps us to learn, and to adjust to a second MVP, etc.

In practical terms, our first experimental carriage could be ready to roll on the line within a couple of weeks. The playbook for the fortnight might look like this:

> check health and safety rules
> communicate and convince key internal stakeholders (station heads, etc.)
> secure 'naked' carriage
> source and install physical components for the carriage (bar, TVs, etc.)
> source drinks (starting with non-alcoholic ones)
> recruit volunteer employees to man the 'FREE TRAVEL' booths
> prepare and refine the script used by the volunteers
> make in-station banners
> etc.

As you can see, the playbook of a Lean Startup experiment is usually a lot fiddlier in practice than the simple Build–Measure–Learn feedback loop would lead us to expect. Don't be disheartened, though. A couple of hours setting the playbook is usually all it takes. And that pales into insignificance compared to the cost of launching a new idea without running an experiment at all, and subsequently falling flat on your face.

On a final note, we alluded earlier to the fact that not all publicity is good publicity if you're an established business. My third tip was to add a layer of hide-ability or deniability to your experiment. Not by lying or obfuscating, but by being smarter and thinking again about what would make your test less likely to be subject to negative publicity. In our example here, the key reputation risk would be if the tests resulted in a few too many incidents of drunkenness.

How could we smartly mitigate our image risk?

Maybe by partnering with an organization for whom incidents of drunkenness would not negatively impact their brand. Like a pub chain or a drinks company. Imagine if our carriage was called the Heineken Carriage, or the Flyin' Wetherspoon. Any media coverage that revealed incidents of excessive drunkenness in this carriage would be laughed out of the room; what did you expect from a bar?!

How would we get Heineken or Wetherspoon to participate in our test? By offering them a very valuable exclusivity of supply for a year, if the test works out and the carriage is rolled out across our whole network. We know that what we're doing here is testing a possible new business unit (i.e. third-class, standing-room-only carriage) and we tell Heineken as much. We also realize – and say so – that various issues might lead to this not working, and we might have to cancel the test after a few weeks or a few months. In the worst-case scenario, where the test is aborted early (and possibly deemed a failure), both Heineken and Avanti could claim that it was just a marketing gimmick, a promotional stunt (by Heineken), and like all such activity, it was intended to have a short shelf life from the start. Using Heineken marketing collaterals that are not meant to last would clearly reinforce the story. In practice, we might start with only Heineken banners in the carriage, before maybe painting the carriage after a few weeks – if the experiment is proving successful so far.

IN SUMMARY

So, in conclusion to this long example, we've seen the amount of detail and careful thinking that goes into planning a session of testing with

Lean, in practice. Time is money. The longer you spend carefully plotting your sequence of tests, the cheaper each one turns out. Conversely, the less time you spend planning, the more expensive everything becomes.

. As a final tip, I often ask clients how they would undertake a given test for a tenth of the cash they are allocating to it so far. Shrinking the budget by 90 per cent does focus the mind brilliantly. Usually, people do come up with a new version of the test (that may not be 90 per cent cheaper, but still 75 per cent cheaper). The most successful way to save cash on tests is by ruthlessly focusing on testing only one critical challenge at a time. There may not be many ways to test four things at the same time, but there are usually many cheap ways to test one challenge at a time. For example, testing that people like your food doesn't require a full-blown restaurant – a simple picnic in the park might do.

As a side benefit, shrinking the amount of cash at risk for every test does help to change a company's culture over time. Tests are less problematic to approve and underwrite if they cost barely anything. Shifting the culture from a traditional 'failure is not an option' mode to 'failure is a very cheap and low-risk way to gather insight'.

The core principle of Lean Startup – test and learn – is brilliant and very simple. It is, however, fiendishly finicky to deploy in practice – but practice makes perfect, and the prize is well worth it.

Lean Startup exercise: How to re-size Holland?

The Lean Startup approach is a great technique to quickly test ideas. Any idea, or at least most ideas. All you need to do is think really hard about which critical hypotheses you are trying to test, and what hideable MVPs will get you the data you need for a pass or a fail. The Lean approach does not come with as structured a method as some of the other strategic techniques. My one key piece of advice is to concentrate on 'sharp data' rather than 'big data'. If the idea we have in mind fails, and we debrief that failure in a few months' time, what can we sense already, today, might be the most likely reason for the failure? That is precisely where one needs to focus the testing right away. Run towards the points of likeliest failure, rather than leave them to last.

Imagine you are working for the Dutch Ministry of Health, Welfare and Sport. They are concerned that however fit the Dutch are in general, they are slowly putting on weight on average – the way most Western societies are. An 'Up' thinking session delivered many great potential ideas to help curtail this, or even reverse the trend. One idea, in particular, feels worth testing right away: paying citizens to lose weight. They would become richer by becoming healthier – and slimmer too in the process.

Hema, a generalist retailer with 500 stores and a clothing offering, would love to get involved. Rather than giving people hard cash, Hema might suggest offering them a clothes voucher, to allow them to buy new clothes, one size smaller, which they will need when they've achieved their goal. Hema and the Dutch Ministry of Health, Welfare and Sport might call this potential campaign 'Re-Sizing Holland', to touch upon both the shrinking of the girth and the shrinking of the clothes. Please note the same campaign might shortly involve Walmart and the US Department of Health and Human Services, or Tesco and the UK Department of Health and Social Care, etc.

Let's pretend we are in the early stages of the project, and two small teams have been asked to think things through on their own first. Each has been asked to identify the critical hypotheses, or critical questions to address, and to prepare a possible test of hide-able MVPs for each.

We have two exercises for you to practise your Lean skills now, and we invite you to share your solutions on www.strategic.how/lean:

> **Lean Startup exercise #1**
  which of Annelieke's team or Klaasjan's team has the best
  plan to test the idea at this stage?

> **Lean Startup exercise #2:**
  what would be your own combination of critical hypotheses
  and tests?

LEAN STARTUP EXERCISE #1:
ANNELIEKE'S TEAM VS. KLAASJAN'S TEAM

Annelieke's Team

Critical Hypotheses	Hideable MPV Test
What % of people want to lose weight?	Survey with 2 questions, asked on the street to 100 people: are you happy with your weight? And would you participate in a national weight-loss challenge?
What is the best incentive scheme?	A/B testing 5 angles in parallel: straight cash, discount vouchers, role models, game, and free clothes.
How long can participants stay motivated/engaged?	Pilot programme run in 1 out-of-the-way store. Supported by app
How do we measure weight (to avoid cheating/fraud)?	?

Klaasjan's's Team

Critical Hypotheses	Hideable MPV Test
What % of people could be incentivized to lose weight?	• 3 days to enlist 1,000 people • 5 shops + 5 gyms • follow up 1 month later
What is the required amount of euros per kilo?	• give people €50 vouchers, and ask them how much weight they've lost only when they spend the voucher
How much is each participant likely to spend at Hema?	• track over 3 months

LEAN STARTUP EXERCISE #2:
YOUR TAKE ON RE-SIZING HOLLAND

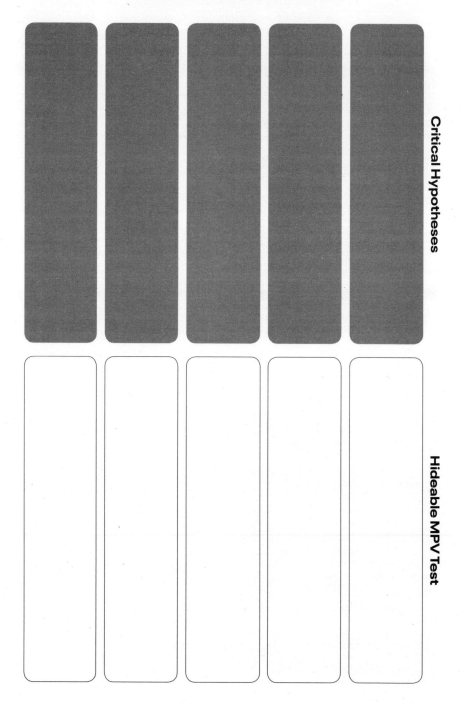

Critical Hypotheses

Hideable MPV Test

PART FOUR

HOW TO GET THE BEST SOLUTION APPROVED ('PUSH')

There are many ways to get from Certainty to Conviction in a business context, and we mentioned in **How to Solve Complex Problems** ('Think'), that you could:

> harness **impactful words** to adapt your communication to the demonstrated individual preference of each stakeholder
> collate some **simple numbers**, as no idea ever gets approved without overcoming some sort of quantitative hurdle, and
> craft a **compelling story** to grab your stakeholders' attention for the key aspects of your recommendation that they need to understand.

In this part, **How to Get the Best Solution Approved** ('Push'), we'll go over two techniques from each family:

> some **impactful words**, with **NLP Language** and **10 Ways to Convince**
> some **simple numbers**, with **Memorable Metrics** and **Pocket NPV**, and
> a **compelling story** with **Pyramid Principle** and **Adland Swagger.**

In the Rollercoaster of Strategic Thinking, 'Push' is the moment when you try to convince others of the validity of your recommended solution. You want them to buy into your solution. You want to get their buy-in. All different ways to express the same thing: you want them to agree with you.

Before we expand further, why don't you 'flip' the issue for a second? Imagine that someone else is trying to get *you* to agree with *them.* What would get *you* to agree to *their* recommendation? Whether the person wanting you to agree with them is your romantic partner, your boss, a supplier, a colleague, a car dealer, etc.

When someone else asks *you* to agree with *them*, they are actually asking you for a leap of faith towards their vision for the future. They are asking you to believe that the answer they have thought of will prove to be the best possible outcome for both parties, in the real world, in a little while (be it in a few seconds, a few years, and all the way to a few decades). When asked what they need in order to believe in such a future outcome – an outcome they can't yet see or touch – humans throughout history have said: 'A compelling story, with some impactful words, and a few simple numbers.' Hence the structure for this 'Push' section.

The challenge when presenting a recommendation for any strategic issue in business is the comparatively thin layer of data. When there isn't much data to share, you have to be more efficient with your numbers, more powerful with your words – and more compelling with your story!

8.

IMPACTFUL WORDS

NLP Language

Neuro-Linguistic Programming (NLP) is a vast movement of practitioners who define their focus as the study of human excellence. They attempt to discover what unique strategies make some people more successful than others. As part of their efforts, they've uncovered something very insightful about language, and communication.

If we take a step back, we can all recognize that we each take on the world through our senses. We see stuff, we hear stuff, we smell stuff, we taste stuff, and we touch stuff. The five senses are the channels by which external information comes to our brains, and allows us to construct a representation of the world in our minds. NLP calls these our five 'representation systems'. NLP then adds a sixth channel, which is the sense for facts and data. Having discovered this channel in the early 1970s, NLP labelled it at the time the 'digital' channel. Digital is a term that holds a lot more meaning these days, but the relevance is still broadly right, being about the processing of bite-size facts and data.

In order to keep things simple, NLP often combines the three most physical senses (touch, smell, taste) into one, and calls them jointly the 'kinaesthetic' channel.

Visual: see + watch
Auditory: hear + speak
Kinaesthetic: grasp + feel
Digital: read + count

So at this point, we have a model for processing information that says that the outside world gets into your brain through four channels: the visual channel (seeing stuff), the auditory channel (hearing and saying stuff), the kinaesthetic channel (feeling and touching stuff) and the digital channel (reading and analysing stuff).

The next big insight from NLP is staggering: most people have a very strong preference for two out of these four channels.

What this means in practice is that, if information reaches someone in a format that matches one of their preferred channels, then the information will hit them much faster, be processed more quickly, and will be that much more convincing. Any information presented in someone's least favourite channel(s) will take longer to reach them, take longer to process, and will strike them as less convincing.

For example, people with the visual channel as one of their preferred channels prefer to see and watch as a way to gather information and be convinced. People with a preference for the auditory channel prefer to hear and speak. Highly kinaesthetic people like to grasp and feel, and highly digital people like to read and count.

You may already know or feel how some channels work better for you than others. If you regularly read documents aloud to yourself, then auditory works better for you than digital. If you switch off the radio when you have to do some parallel parking in the car, then visual works better for you than auditory, etc.

Most people subconsciously know what channels work best for them, and they walk around oozing that fact to the world. It's impossible to spot in others if you don't know what to pay attention to, and it's impossible to miss in others when you know what the clues are.

It turns out that the words people use are massive clues. Each one of us uses language that is highly skewed towards words from our preferred representation system. We signal to the world what channels we would like the world to use with us, and we do so by the words we use. The four tables below offer a selection of words and expressions that clearly belong to specific representation systems.

Once you know someone's preferred channels, using more language from those channels will reach their hearts and minds more directly, and will convince them faster and better of the validity of your recommended solution to any problem.

VISUAL SYSTEM

Highly visual people like to use visual language. They'll use words like see, focus, clear, bright, picture, hazy, etc. Visual people ooze visual language. Once you notice that someone uses a lot of visual language, you have a clue as to how to interact better with them. First, use visual language yourself, and then provide a lot more visual stimulus – whether through slides, or presentations, or pictures – because they'll prefer to see something and watch it in order to gather information and be convinced.

Typical words	Typical expressions
> See	> 'I get the picture'
> Focus	> 'It's clear now'
> Clear	> 'I see what you mean'
> Bright	> 'Things are looking up'
> Picture	> 'I take a dim view of that'
> Hazy	> 'The outlook is bleak'
> Colour	> 'Things are a bit hazy'
> View	> 'We've got a clear way forward'
> Dim	> 'That's a colourful expression'
> Look	> 'He's in a black mood today'
	> 'Looks good to me'
	> 'Seeing eye to eye'
	> 'Shed light on it'
	> 'Colourful show'
	> 'Big picture'

AUDITORY SYSTEM

Auditory people use a lot of auditory language. Words like sound, hear, tell, say, etc., and slightly noisier sounds, like click, bang, etc. They might use expressions like 'I tell myself', 'Listen to yourself', or 'We're singing from the shame hymn sheet', etc. They use a lot of language that refers to sounds, spoken and heard. Once you decipher that, one of the ways you can interact with them better is by using lots of such language yourself, and talking to them. And listening. And talking.

Typical words	Typical expressions
› Sound	› 'I tell myself to take care'
› Hear	› 'Tell me how it is'
› Tell	› 'Things clicked into place'
› Say	› 'Let me explain'
› Click	› 'We're in harmony'
› Bang	› 'Listen to yourself'
› Talk	› 'We're in tune with each other'
› Volume	› 'It was music to my ears'
› Loud	› 'I'm pleased you said that'
› Snap	› 'I'm glad to hear it'
	› 'Sounds right to me'
	› 'Can't hear myself think'
	› 'Singing our tune'
	› 'Clear explanation'
	› 'Rings a bell'

People who have a strong auditory preference need to talk things through. They might often completely ignore your well-put-together slides or memos, and insist on starting from scratch with a chat. If you have a lot of props (photos, objects, etc.), leave these aside and talk to them, engage them with words. Auditory people want to hear, and they want to speak in return.

KINAESTHETIC SYSTEM

Kinaesthetic people like to grasp and feel. They use vocabulary like impact, feel, grasp, tense, rough, relax, etc. All sorts of very physical vocabulary or emotional vocabulary. First use similar vocabulary, and second try to communicate with them through experiences, interactions and emotions. Do an exercise with them, get them to stand up, to walk around, to maybe hug or high-five, or do something a bit more physical, because that reaches their core better than images or sounds.

Typical words	Typical expressions
› Impact	› 'Racked with pain'
› Feel	› 'Sweet smell of success'
› Grasp	› 'In touch with reality'
› Tense	› 'I grasp what you mean'
› Rough	› 'I've got a handle on it'
› Relaxed	› 'Warm regards'
› Firm	› 'It was a blow to me'
› Pressure	› 'Let's firm up on this'
› Tackle	› 'He savoured the moment'
› Weigh	› 'Hold on'
	› 'Feels good'
	› 'Heated debate'
	› 'Smell a rat'

DIGITAL SYSTEM

Finally, we find people who have a strong digital preference – a very common type in any business context. They'd rather read and count, and the vocabulary they use includes words like accommodate, capability, comprehend, etc., and most words with three or more syllables. Digital people can be a bit dry, and can sometimes come across as a bit robotic to the other types. Offering no images for the visual, no stories for the auditory, and no emotions for the kinaesthetic. Digital types communicate without much poetry, and that's how they like it. Match them for structure and facts, and they're more likely to be convinced.

Typical words	Typical expressions
> Accommodate	> 'These things don't add up'
> Capability	> 'This makes sense'
> Comprehend	> 'Regarding your concern'
> Establish	> 'Considering possibilities'
> Hypothesize	> 'An interesting dilemma'
> Judge	> 'A viable solution'
> Ponder	> 'Analyse the potential'
> Qualify	> 'Evaluate the options'
> Think	> 'Value quality'
> Most words with 3+ syllables!	> 'Promote a philosophy'
	> 'A downsizing is indicated'

IN SUMMARY

NLP Language offers multiple avenues to convince others. Pay attention to the vocabulary people use, because the system they use the most (visual, auditory, kinaesthetic, digital) is an indication of the channel they prefer when receiving their information from you. Then use language from that channel – and the relevant selection of pictures, debates, stories and numbers – to carry the day.

For more details on this, see my old boss and first NLP teacher, Julian Vyner, and his great book *Mastering Soft Skills: Win and Build Better Client Relationships with a New Approach to Influence, Persuasion and Selling.*

As a final illustration, consider the worlds that Apple and Amazon have built. Influenced by Steve Jobs and Jony Ive, the Apple world is visually stunning and very kinaesthetic. From the dancing shapes in the original iPod ads, to the wood in the Apple Stores, and the rounded angle of apps in the App Store, etc., everything Apple does is very strongly visual-kinaesthetic. Browse through Amazon's website instead, and everything looks and feels less Zen. The drop-down menus with zillions of options, the search results that scream different words at you, etc. A lot of the Amazon universe comes across as strongly auditory-digital.

NLP Language example

We've mentioned so far that most people have a strong preference for two representation systems. In order to keep things simple here, let's construct four archetypal individuals with *only one* preferred channel each. A visual person, an auditory person, a digital person and a kinaesthetic person. Instead of having them walk into a bar, let's have them walk into an Audi showroom on a Tuesday afternoon. The showroom is located on one of the most prestigious avenues in town, and cars cannot be taken out for a test drive. Let's examine how each of our four characters would prefer to interact with the sales people in the showroom.

First, the visual person walks into the showroom. The salesman approaches and asks, 'Can I help you at all?' The visual person says, 'No thank you, I'm just looking.' And in their mind they are thinking, 'And that's why I went out of my way to avoid making eye contact with you!' With their strong preference for taking in as much visual information as possible, the visual person would usually rather not be bothered by the chatty sales rep. From experience, the visual person knows that reps will mostly deliver a long string of words, far less useful than a good browse. Far better to send the rep packing right away. If need be, there will always be the possibility to wave towards him when in need of a specific piece of information.

Now an auditory person walks into the showroom. The salesman approaches and asks, 'Can I help you at all?' The auditory person says, 'Yes please, tell me about your cars.' It has sometimes been observed at that point that, when standing in front of the car, the auditory person might turn their back on the car, in order to face the salesperson. An order of preference that might baffle most non-auditory people. In some instances, hearing more footsteps behind them, the auditory customer might turn round, spot another sales rep passing by, and ask them to join the conversation as well. The resulting situation is an auditory person's dream: two people talking to you at once, and voicing slightly different opinions to help you choose a course of action. This setup is many a non-auditory person's idea of hell!

Next, imagine a digital person walks into the showroom. The salesman approaches and asks, 'Can I help you at all?' The digital person might start their reply with either yes or no, but the key component of it will often be, 'I just want some brochures,' or, 'Some information that I can't find online.' It has been observed that some digital people would then take the brochure, turn on their heels, and leave. Without looking at the cars, or speaking with the sales reps. The purely visual person would totally understand not speaking with the sales rep, and the purely auditory person would totally understand not looking at the cars, but neither of them can understand just walking away with a brochure.

Finally, a kinaesthetic person walks into the showroom. The salesman approaches and asks, 'Can I help you at all?' Again, the kinaesthetic person might start their reply with yes or no, but more importantly the following words will likely be something like, 'I just want to sit in the car.' Upon hearing that a kinaesthetic person wants to sit in a stationary car, a digital person might think, 'What a great idea to gather additional data towards assessing the suitability of this car as a future purchase.' Another kinaesthetic person instead, upon hearing that someone wants to sit in a stationary car, might feel, 'Oh, that must have felt nice!'

The visual person wants to look at the cars first and foremost, the auditory person wants to talk about them with someone else, the digital person wants to read and analyse information, and the kinaesthetic person wants to experience, touch and feel the car.

Each of these four individuals will be all the more convinced by

a given car if they can receive the information they need through the NLP channel(s) they prefer.

Any sales rep who understands the importance of NLP channels will go out of their way to give customers information in channels that the customers prefer. An old-fashioned salesperson, however, will probably only focus on their own preferred channel rather than their customers'. Unsurprisingly, the most popular channel among sales reps is the auditory channel. A more sophisticated salesman will ask a few questions to quickly ascertain the customer's preferred channels, and will then pivot the main mode of communication towards these channels.

A really advanced NLP practitioner will even know how to spot someone's representation channel before needing to talk to them. It can be inferred reasonably reliably from the way people walk, or dress, or generally interact with their surroundings. In other words, it can be noticed from afar, which allows you to decide how best to interact with people, well before the first hello.

Imagine now that the same four customers, each with their own channel preference, enter the showroom at the exact same time, with only one sales rep on duty. There is a clear optimal order in which this sole sales rep should deal with these four customers to maximize everyone's satisfaction, and therefore the opportunity of a sale. Can you take 10 seconds and work out the optimal order? Which customer should the sales rep approach first? Visual, auditory, kinaesthetic, or digital?

The first customer to approach is clearly the auditory one. It's the only one of the four customers who genuinely wants to talk to the sales rep. The other three are neutral at best, and some might even be hostile to chatting with the rep. Now what should the rep say to the auditory customer?

The right answer is not, 'Can I help you at all?' Since the rep has already worked out that the customer is auditory, the right first sentence should be something like, 'Let's talk about my cars! Could you give me one minute first, to deal with these three customers? I know what they want to ask me and I'll be back with you right away and we can speak at length. By the way, would you like coffee, and how do you take it?' We know that the other three customers are less keen on interacting with the rep than the auditory one, and therefore the rep might indeed be back chatting with the auditory customer very shortly. Who should the rep turn to next?

Probably the digital customer. We know that a digital customer would have a strong preference for reading and analysing information without distraction. The easiest thing for the rep to help with that would be to point, from a few metres away, to a table on which multiple brochures and leaflets are available for consumption. Sometimes not even speaking with the digital customer is more enjoyable for them.

Between the remaining two customers, the visual and the kinaes-thetic, who should the rep turn to next? Clearly the kinaesthetic. We know the visual person would rather not be interfered with at all! They would rather browse and peruse at their leisure. When a highly visual person needs additional information from, or interaction with, a rep, they typically wave their arms above their head, in silence, possibly including a hand gesture for the rep to come their way. (Please note that an auditory person in the same circumstances might just shout across the room, 'Excuse me, can you help me?') So at this stage the rep leaves the visual person well alone.

Walking towards the kinaesthetic person, the rep starts by shaking hands, possibly putting his other hand on the customer's shoulder or elbow. He then explains that all the cars are for sitting in, and that the customer should feel free to take their time. The rep then disappears, to go back to the auditory person. It is not uncommon for a kinaesthetic person to then slide into the seat, and play with all the buttons and handles in the car, confident that the rep won't be back to disturb them for a while.

Surveying his showroom, our rep can feel proud of a job well done. Three of his customers are absorbing huge amounts of information in the fashion that they each prefer. Walking back towards the auditory customer waiting by the entrance the rep has two choices: go make the coffee and then engage the customer in conversation, or grab the cus-tomer, walk with them to the kitchen and start to talk in the noisy environment of this small, windowless and smelly room. Now that you understand the essence of representation systems and channels, you know that the auditory customer (and only this customer!) would prefer chatting in the noisy, manky kitchen rather than read, touch or look at cars on their own.

It is reasonably easy to understand why Audi showrooms look the way they look, and so do the showrooms of many a luxury car brand. Where should the sales rep desk be? As far away from the entrance to the showroom as possible. Why? Two reasons. First, to allow reps to observe customers from afar for a few seconds, in order to guess their preferred representation system, and start approaching them in their preferred channel (or leave the visuals alone!). Second, because with the exception of auditory types, most customers are ambivalent about sales reps. Leaving as much distance as possible between the entrance and sales rep desk is a way to subliminally influence the other three types that they won't be pestered by the reps – or at least not too much, or not too soon.

When it comes to the layout of the room, you can probably easily understand why there is often a table near the entrance, with lots of brochures and various information sheets. The driver's door of about half the cars is in the opened position. And the cars are not aligned in a visually boring straight line, but rather in an apparently haphazard zig-zag way, with a surprising new angle on every step.

The best way to ensure that a varied selection of customers is convinced by what you have to offer, be it a car or a recommended business solution, is to blend the four representation systems in your presentation. Nowhere does it matter more than in the executive summary of the pitch for a brand-new idea or venture, as we'll see shortly.

10 Ways to Convince

The 4 channels of NLP Language highlight the importance of the *format* of the words one can use to influence others, and the 10 Ways to Convince model focuses on the *nature* of these words.

The first way to convince is **Reason**. It is the way to convince most commonly used by strategists and strategy consultants. They typically default to rational arguments, for example: 'Here are three excellent reasons why you should do X, Y, Z.' It works beautifully, in particular if you do happen to have a solid argument to back it up. It's a bit less effective if the evidence is weak, or if the recipient finds the evidence weak.

The use of reason as a way to convince can be made using visual, auditory, kinaesthetic or digital language. Yes, there is a tendency to use digital language to support a highly rational approach – but it need not be automatic. All nine other ways to convince can similarly be expressed via all four NLP channels, while having perhaps a stronger affinity with one or two of them.

The second way to convince is **Ask**. Typically: 'Would you like to be rich?' We're not putting rationality behind this; we are using a leading question to get the recipients to convince themselves, so that they feel responsible for the decision. Asking someone, 'How would you make this work?' is a great way to 'flip' them from a defensive stance, where they count on you to convince them, into a participative stance, where they work with you to convince themselves.

A third way to convince is **Authority**. 'It's our policy not to refund cash.' Not very effective when you deal with senior-level board executives and you're an external consultant, but employed sometimes without noticing it by lots of people towards their juniors. Authority does work well in some specific circumstances, like when you're running out of time, or there are too many voices being heard. It can cut both ways, though, and it usually only works with the most compliant members of the audience, who are not always the most strategic.

A fourth way would be **Force**. 'The last person only lasted two weeks. You do it.' We don't always acknowledge that we use that approach. However, most people do. If you think back on your career, you will have seen people using it. If you were to ask these people, in turn, whether they used force, they might demur, and say not really, even though they might regularly do so.

The fifth way is **Expertise**. 'In my experience', etc. A very useful way to convince, especially if the problem at hand has happened before, and the person doing the talking can point to some relevant expertise. One slight drawback of over-playing the expert card is that it is heavily focused on past experiences and present knowledge, and may sound ancient to more future-oriented, disrupter types.

The five ways to convince that we've seen so far share a common trait: they very much come from the head, rather than the heart. Reason, Ask, Authority, Force and Expertise are all somewhat clinical, and devoid of emotion. The next Five Ways we'll see now are warmer, tugging a bit more at the heart rather than appealing to the head.

Reason	**Inspire**
Ask	**Silent Allies**
Authority	**Feel Good**
Force	**Deal**
Expertise	**Favour**

The sixth way to convince is **Inspire**. Emotional persuasion: 'Once more unto the breach, dear friends!' Or, 'Let's do it!' Or, 'Build the future with me and this venture!' Many of us will actually use that a lot in our personal lives, and slightly refrain from doing so in a professional context. Everything you hear or read will have made you aware of the importance of emotional intelligence (eQ) and getting people on board. Inspiring may not be as pleasant as rationality to highly analytical minds, but it does work.

Our seventh way to convince is **Silent Allies**. Which is something like: 'eight out of ten people prefer', or 'all our competitors', etc. This is something quite a few people use all the time, in personal or business contexts. The power of the silent allies way to convince is the reason why benchmarking, grading, league tables, etc. are so popular. Every human being loves a bit of comparison. When you recommend a new solution to an audience, being able to compare it to similar things done by similar people is a great way to reassure – and thus convince.

The eighth way is **Feel Good**. 'You did really well on this particular project', 'I'm really proud of you', 'We think you're amazing'. A lot of you will be uncomfortable with that, equating feel good with unwarranted flattery. Before you dismiss it out of hand, outright flattery has been a core component of getting powerful people to do what you want, from Machiavelli's 'Prince' onwards. Feel good may not feel morally right, but it works brilliantly as a way to convince. Oh, and most parents use it with their kids regularly!

The ninth way is **Deal**. 'If you do this for me, I'll do this for you.' You scratch my back, I scratch your back. Absolutely no need for reason to underpin that, just a straightforward deal. A lot of businesspeople who move into politics, in particular, find that their inability to do deals of that nature impedes them in the political context. Because in the political arena these deals are the stock in trade, the normal way for anyone to elicit other people's backing. 'You help fund my school, I help fund your hospital.' No reason, force, expertise, silent allies, etc., just a straightforward deal.

The final way to convince is **Favour**: emotional appeal. 'I'd really like it if you did X, Y, Z', 'Could you do this for me?', etc. It is a subtle way to appeal to people's kindness rather than their analytical mind. The recipient of the favour request might still process it analytically through other ways to convince. (Reason: 'Does the request make sense?' Deal: 'What do I get in exchange?', etc.) Asking for a favour, however, is a great way to remove early heat from the conversation.

I often sit in training sessions with participants, asking them to think about these ten methods, and to identify the three they most commonly use. Because I usually work with strategists or senior executives, reason comes out quite high and then we'll get a few others. We might get a bit of inspire and a bit of ask, we'll definitely have authority, we'll have a few people who do deals, and the other methods are less prevalent. Eight out of 10 people who look at this acknowledge that they do have three or four preferred ways to convince that they fall back on all the time. Ask yourself this: would you rather drive a four-cylinder car or an eight-cylinder car? Most people work on four cylinders, using four ways to convince. If you can broaden that to eight or 10, that would be extraordinary. You could convince lots more people. Have a go! What do you have to lose?

A simple, practical way to broaden your range is mimicry. Which friend, relative or colleague of yours do you think of when you consider the use of expertise, or feel good, or favour, etc.? Every human being has a different set of preferences among these 10 Ways to Convince. Consequently, all of us have in our immediate social circle people with preferences markedly different from ours. As a clue, it's usually people you won't find very convincing . . . because they don't typically use your own favourite way to convince! When it comes to convincing others, a great way to broaden your range is to practise the art of conviction using your least favourite ways to convince . . . and notice how people can, and do, get convinced by these! Why does this work? Because not everyone is like you. Your least favourite ways to convince are music to someone else's ears . . . and vice versa.

Impactful Words exercise: How to pitch a new venture?

There are tons of resources out there to help you write great presentations, and all of them say the same thing about the executive summary. Keep it short, make it punchy, grab the attention, summarize the key elements of your idea in one to three pages maximum.

That's great. But what if you need to grab someone's attention in under one second? Then flyers are still the holy grail. As used by comedians at the Edinburgh Festival, or anyone standing in the path of someone else in a public place. A flyer has one second to grab your attention, otherwise it ends up on the road or in the bin. Let's have a look at writing an executive summary like a great flyer.

First, may I suggest to you that an executive summary is one page. One page only. Not two, not three. Don't make people flip over, just one page. Second, somewhere at the top of the page you put a great slogan, in big letters, with bold colours. Let's look at an example of an online pharmacy. Online Pharmacy is the name of the business, or the venture, and then 'Meds On Tap' is its slogan.

The third component is a stunning, memorable photo. Something quite visual that will attract the eye. The fourth tip is a bit more kinaesthetic. Put super-short bios of the two, three or four key people who will execute on that plan / pitch / initiative, etc.

The fifth tip is to include maybe three key metrics. A metric with the amount of upfront investment required, a second metric that will be key to operational success, and a third metric of financial return. The final tip is, don't use more than 300 words. Aim for between 200 and 300 words max. And make sure that you highlight different bits of the text.

Because each one of us reads diagonally when something arrives in our inbox, or on our desk. We all do that naturally. The recipient will do it for your summary, the same way you do it for other people's communications.

What you end up with is something like the one-pager below. Hopefully this discussion here on executive summary has stayed within two minutes.

To quickly summarize: one page that looks like a flyer, that really attracts the attention of the readers, engages them into further reading, and can be left on their desk or their wall afterwards as a reminder of your communication.

Do share your one-page executive summary of new venture pitches on www.strategic.how/words and we'll gladly offer feedback. Forcing yourself to condense weeks of work into one sole page is a great exercise in impactful words.

WORDS EXERCISE:
ONE-PAGE EXECUTIVE SUMMARY

The Online Pharmacy 'Meds on Tap'

John Reeleaf
CEO
15 years at Walgreens
MBA Harvard

Kelly O'Kiefe,
Chief Pharmacist
12 years at CVS
PharmD, Ohio State

Phil Washington
Ops Director
8 years at Amazon
3 years at eBay

$2.5m
Initial Investment

3,000
Customers by Year 3

30%
Return on Investment

The Online Pharmacy's main goal is to **provide prescription medications** for our customers at the **lowest prices** on the market. We will be able to sell prescriptions at reduced prices by carefully maintaining efficiencies in our operations and by targeting a specific segment of the market — those **customers who pay for their prescriptions medications themselves.**

Focusing on this segment it gives us real **operational efficiencies.** We avoid disruptions in cash flow often associated with insurance payments and we can eliminate unnecessary services for the types of **knowledgeable, repeat customer** taking maintenance-type medication.

The Online Pharmacy will operate from **one warehouse** that will serve both internet and phone customers. We will thrive by employing **friendly and knowledgeable personnel,** which, along with our great prices, will drive the repeat business that we will rely upon.

We only expect that as the price of medication continues to skyrocket, The Online Pharmacy will appeal more and more to the customer's sense of value and convenience. Our advertising, mainly through ads in sites for the **over-55 crowd,** will be targeted at those who are looking to **save money** on a pricey but necessary and regular expense.

The Online Pharmacy will be led by **John Reeleaf,** an MBA with **15 years experience** in the pharmaceutical industry. Costs will be minimized by maintaining only one pharmacist and multiple pharmaceutical techs. We expect to reach **profitability by our second year** and will generate substantial sales by year three.

9.

SIMPLE NUMBERS

Memorable Metrics

Convincing others to do something new in a business context always involves some kind of numbers. These numbers don't have to be complicated, but they have to be memorable. Two of the most commonly used sentences in management are 'What gets measured gets managed' and 'Measure drives behaviour'. Both hit on the importance of data and measurement in business, each with a different twist.

'What gets measured gets managed' is looking more directly at the present. It suggests that the best way to get something done, or managed, is to create a measure for it. It's a tactical tip. Put *any measure* on someone's to do list and the desired outcome is more likely to be achieved over time, now that someone is monitoring it. Anybody who's ever run a team understands the wisdom of this.

'Measure drives behaviour' looks a bit further into the future. It suggests that what you choose to measure will have an impact on what people spend their time on, how they do things, etc. It's a strategic tip. Choose *which measure* to prioritize and watch people behave differently as they align the company to a new direction over time. Whether you use carrots, sticks, or a mix of both, you can drive a large change of direction by regularly updating what you decide to measure.

A very effective way to convince others with data is to identify the most important factors for success, and highlight how these will change positively over the period of the project or initiative you recommend. One can use many names for that, such as key performance indicators, dashboard, etc. Kaplan and Norton introduce the notion of the Balanced Scorecard, as a way to concentrate in one place all these measures for success. Broadly speaking, these are the Memorable Metrics necessary for driving safely towards your desired future.

Most decision making revolves around financial data. And good financial data is historical in nature. So Kaplan and Norton suggest that driving a business using only financial statements is a bit like driving a car using only the rear-view mirror: difficult and dangerous. Financial information is a lagging indicator of good fortune.

Compare, for example, the time lag in a restaurant between the information a cook and a waitress see, when it comes to how well the restaurant is doing. The waitress knows right away how well the restaurant is likely to be doing that evening, by seeing how many tables are occupied. The cook will only notice the same information with a 15-minute time lag, when the orders start coming in. An absentee owner might even lag behind by a few more hours, if receiving the financial data only at the end of the evening.

Following on from this, Kaplan and Norton suggest adding three new perspectives, in addition to the financial perspective, to help drive your activity better: the customer perspective, the business process perspective, and the learning and growth perspective.

Note that these four perspectives are relevant for any company as a whole, as well as for departments, or teams (whose customers might be other internal functions or teams). The Kaplan Norton Balanced Scorecard suggests that anyone, or any activity, will succeed better if keeping an eye on four perspectives. Let's address them in turn.

> **Financial perspective:** timely and accurate financial data will always be a priority to successfully manage established businesses and pilot new ones. There is often, however, more than enough handling and processing of financial data, and sole emphasis on pure financials leads to the 'unbalanced' situation. One could perhaps include additional financial-related data, such as risk assessment and cost-benefit data, but the most critical next step is to turn to the other three perspectives.

> **Customer perspective:** customer focus and customer satisfaction are hugely important in any business, and especially new ones. These are leading indicators. If customers are not satisfied, they will eventually find other suppliers that will

meet their needs. Poor performance from the customer perspective is thus a leading indicator of future decline, even though the current financial picture may look good.

> **Business process perspective:** metrics based on this perspective allow any manager to know how well their business is running, and whether its products and services conform to current and future customer requirements. These metrics have to be carefully designed by those who know the processes most intimately.

> **Learning and growth perspective:** includes employee training and corporate cultural attitudes related to both individual and corporate self-improvement. In a twenty-first-century organization, people are often the main resource, and they should be in a continuous learning mode. Learning is more than just training; it also includes things like mentors, tutors, knowledge-sharing processes, and tools. For the company itself, it includes any source of renewal and expansion, like R&D, intellectual property, etc.

Once one understands the four perspectives, it is easy to work out how using only the financial perspective offers a limited view of success, of how to achieve it, and how to retain it. Let's illustrate that with a streaming service – be it Netflix, or Prime Video, or Disney+, etc. Imagine that you're the CEO, and ask yourself, what are the 12 metrics, across four perspectives, that you should be measuring to navigate your business safely to the sustainable and profitable future that you hope is around the corner? The financial measures are the usual suspects: revenues, costs, cash. How about the other ones? Here is a possible scorecard for Netflix today.

Let's focus on the process measures. When Netflix was launched, in 1997, it was simply a mail-order business for film DVDs. The percentage of despatched DVDs that reached customers' actual homes must have been a pretty important process indicator at the time, worth monitoring and managing. Of course, this issue has now completely disappeared, but it stayed at the top of the pile for nearly 10 years. In 2007, Netflix launched its streaming service and, all of a sudden, issues like server downtime, software bug resolution speed, etc. became more critical. Bring that forward another decade and the key process issues for Netflix centre a lot more on the inventory of films and series available to stream than they do on technological and delivery issues.

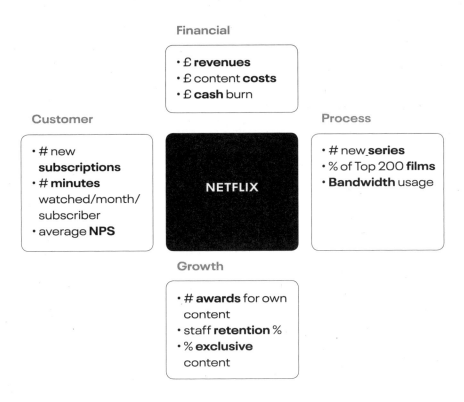

This illustrates one key aspect of Memorable Metrics: prioritize the right ones at the right time. A scorecard, dashboard, etc. can be used both tactically (to manage the current measures) or strategically (to drive new behaviour via new measures). The role of the good strategist is to identify the different measures to use at different stages in the life of any business or new venture, and to retire individual measures when they've become redundant. If all the indicators on the dashboard are bright green, then you are probably not measuring the right things!

Let's use one more illustration, astutely using a scorecard in one's personal life. Imagine that your friend Philippa is planning her life for the next 10 years. In the financial measure box she might write 'salary' as her first indicator. If that's her only metric, then what will she do over the next 10 years? Try to increase her salary. There are two ways to do that: work hard, expect to be recognized for it, and rewarded with promotion and salary increase; or listen to external calls, meet with head hunters, and change firm for a higher salary. Both are perfectly legitimate ways to maximize the Memorable Metric Philippa has set for herself.

Now imagine instead that the metric she chooses for herself is 'salary per hour worked'. This clearly would lead Philippa to adopt different behaviours. She might focus on working smarter rather than on simply working more. She will look for productivity hacks, and she'll start delegating more. If salary is her metric, she'll want to do everything herself and be recognized for it. If salary per hour is her metric instead, then she'd rather delegate a lot, let other people do the work, and let them be recognized for it (so they are happy to work for her again the next time round).

Two lessons emerge from that: first, measure does indeed drive behaviour. Focusing on the salary measure or the salary per hour measure leads to different behaviours. Second, some measures are clearly smarter than others. In our example here, it is not difficult to realize that the behaviour Philippa adopts when focusing on salary per hour is more effective for her employers, her direct reports, and for herself! Not only does she get a better work–life balance by managing her work hours better, she also delivers more benefits to the company through better leveraging her direct reports. That will likely lead to a faster promotion, with the sought-after increase in salary. Win-win-win-win.

A great key to convince others of the validity of a new idea or new venture that you push forward is to select Memorable Metrics that they can see generate behaviours and side benefits that are all conducive to success. And pick a blend of metrics: some for managing the present (for example, salary for Philippa), some for creating a future of better desired outcomes (for example, salary per hour), and others being a lot more aspirational, shifting behaviours for the long term. Imagine, for example, that Philippa now adds 'assets' to her list of financial metrics.

She will start focusing on maximizing assets. This can be achieved inside the company, by chasing ever more important salary increases and stock options. Possibly by sacrificing the salary per hour metric, and working all the hours that she can again. Increased assets can also be achieved outside the company, by keeping salaried hours under control, and dedicating her spare time to investing her existing cash into other ventures. Property, import/export, shares, etc. are all popular ways for people to increase their asset base while still meeting, or even exceeding, their professional obligations to their employers.

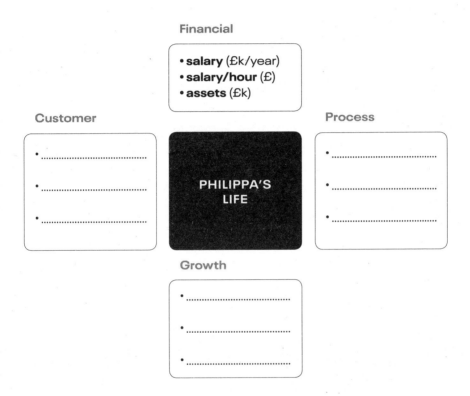

If you pause for a second, and bring this insight to your own life, you might fully embrace how 'measure drives behaviour'. The most effective first step for Philippa (and you) towards building some assets is to emphasize 'assets' as a measure on her (and your) balanced score-card, over 'salary' and 'salary per hour'. If you don't think about a personal objective of yours regularly, you are unlikely to achieve it. And the same applies to organizations as a whole.

When the Balanced Scorecard first came on to the scene, some people and some organizations went a bit overboard. Measuring everything. Creating dashboards with hundreds of measures. The 'What gets measured gets done' school of management. A somewhat more effective way to use balanced scorecards in an organization might be to think of them like Russian dolls. Every person (or function) should have their own scorecard, with a different one for their boss, and a different one for their direct reports – with each scorecard kept quite simple.

Likewise, for a new venture, or a new project, the metrics should be few, simple and memorable. The 'Measure drives behaviour' school of management. Best practice would probably recommend 12 Memorable Metrics, with three in each of the perspectives. A really superb roll-out plan for a new idea might even create a glide path, highlighting which new metrics will be promoted when the current ones become easily met or obsolete (remember the Netflix metrics around postal accuracy becoming server downtime, etc.).

The way to discover your most Memorable Metrics is to come up with dozens of possible metrics at first, across all four perspectives. Then remove all the metrics from the dashboard, and begrudgingly add them back, one by one. Like a supercilious bouncer at a high-end VIP party at the Oscars, you have to decide: if I only let in one metric, which one do I choose? If I only let in two, which one is the next one? And so on. It's a great way to discover which of the metrics create the closest approximation of success for your recommended business solution.

You can find out more about the Balanced Scorecard from the original *Harvard Business Review* article by Robert S. Kaplan and David P. Norton: 'The Balanced Scorecard—Measures that Drive Performance'.

The Balanced Scorecard (or any other similar technique) offers a 'flow' of numbers. Sometimes, a new venture needs to be quantified using a 'stock' of numbers. This is a bit like the difference between speed and destination when driving a car. You input your destination into a GPS app once (a stock of number) and you then watch your speed every few minutes (a flow of numbers) to get you there. The most commonly used 'stock' number is NPV (Net Present Value) and we discuss a pocket version of this right away.

Pocket NPV

NPV (Net Present Value) is a technique for putting a financial value on an initiative, or a business. Many people in your organization's corporate finance department can probably explain it in more detail. In this section, though, I will offer a brief introduction, a formula, and a recipe for arriving at a great outcome without getting lost in the details. Think of it as the pocket version of NPV, rather than the full desktop version. The objective is to put a rough financial value on different options, to help compare them. There are four big principles behind the NPV method:

> **The value of anything is the value of its future flows of cash.**
  For example, imagine that you are a corner shop owner
  looking to add a shelf at the front of your store to sell fresh
  coconuts. The value to you of the 'add coconut shelf'
  initiative is just the sum of all the cash flows you will be
  getting in the future from the sale of these fresh coconuts.
  Cash flows in year 1, year 2, year 3, etc. are usually identified
  by letter CF_1, CF_2, CF_3, etc.

> **Cash in the future is worth less than cash in the present.** If a
  friend who owes you £100 gives it back to you today, and you
  put it in the bank, you might earn interest of £3 or more
  during the year. If your friend waits a whole year before
  reimbursing you instead, you won't be able to earn that
  interest. Therefore, £100 in the future is worth less to you
  than £100 in the present. How much less? We use a discount
  rate, usually labelled r, to bring cash flows from the future
  back to today. This r is a measure of the riskiness of the
  initiative you're valuing. The riskier the initiative, the more
  at risk your future cash flows are, and the higher the discount
  rate. Just like with friends who owe you money, waiting for
  some people to pay you back is riskier than for others!

> **Most initiatives require an upfront investment.** In the coconut
  selling example, you might have to buy some plywood and

hire a carpenter to create a sturdy and attractive shelf, and source an initial stock of coconuts. We refer to this initial cash outlay as K (shorthand for capital).

> **Beyond five years, any forecast is dodgy.** Cash flows become nearly impossible to accurately envisage past a certain time. Instead of continuing with this, we calculate a terminal value (TV), which is just the discounted value of all future cash flows thereafter, assuming no change from year five.

Any corporate finance specialist could at this point very easily spend a few hours, or days, calculating a precise value for any option, with the following formula:

$$\mathbf{NPV} = -\mathbf{K} + \sum_{n=1}^{5} \frac{\mathbf{CF_n}}{\mathbf{(1+r)^n}} + \frac{\mathbf{TV}}{\mathbf{(1+r)^5}}$$

Instead of diving into these calculations, let's spend a few minutes painting a picture. Let's say that you've looked at three options for your organization, and you are now embarking on a financial assessment, trying to work out what is the NPV for each of these options. Before you put hand to laptop and Excel, take pen and paper, and have a go at visually contrasting what you would expect to be the shape of the NPV components for the different options.

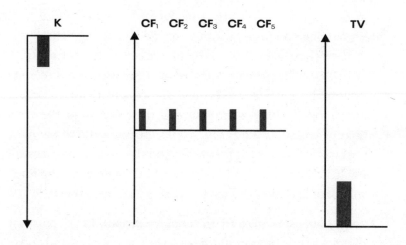

For example, let's start with Option A. First you draw the initial investment, then the cash flows, and finally the terminal value. A good way to roughly estimate TV in five years' time is to ask yourself how much someone else might be willing to pay for your initiative at that time.

Once you have drawn the shape of that first option, turn to Option B (and later Option C) and ask yourself three questions:

> › How does the investment of the second option compare with the investment of the first one? Is it bigger, smaller, much bigger, etc? You are looking for a relative order of magnitude between B and A, rather than an absolute amount. Absolute amounts are hard to find, and are likely to be incorrect. A relative ratio between the options is easier to gauge, and also more likely to be true.

> › What is the difference in the cash flow shapes between the options? Again, instead of putting numbers on that right away, go for an order of magnitude, and then document it visually. Are the cash flows going to be about the same, double, three times bigger, ten times bigger, etc.?

> › Finally, do the same with the terminal value, when you ask yourself not what is the exact terminal value of Option B or Option C, but rather what is the difference in size between the terminal values of the different options?

Is the shape of a given option very traditional, or is there something quirky? Do we have an additional investment in year 3, or do we have a big pay-off at some point (through selling a licence, or something like that), and then the cash flows go down again? With a bit of practice, a simple visual like the picture below helps the team tease out how they understand the shape of each option over the next five years. You ask yourself questions about the shape of the business performance over time, rather than worry about detailed financials. These come later. When finished, you will have achieved something that contains no actual numbers but offers a rich visual contrast between the options.

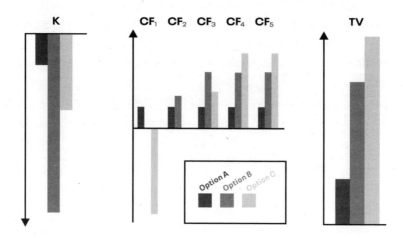

Let's pretend that you do have access to *some* numbers. For example, you know that the initial investment for Option A is likely to be around $2 million. Our picture then implies that the investment for Option B might be roughly $12 million, and $5 million for Option C.

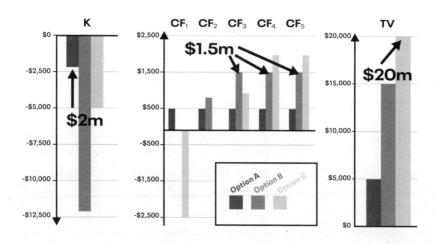

Likewise, if you're pretty sure that the ongoing Option B cash flows from year 3 onwards are roughly $1.5 million, you can then quantify the remaining cash flows, for Option B and the other two options. Same again with the terminal value. Instead of starting by focusing on the actual value of all NPV components for each option, we first create a visual comparison between them. Only once we have completed the picture do we anchor it with whatever limited data we can get access to.

What you end up with is a very visual sense of how each option behaves. How they start, how they progress, and how they end. It's better to have really understood what's going to happen to the business before you put hand to Excel. A very common mistake is to spend a lot of time creating a spreadsheet, putting in all the numbers, and then realizing a little bit too late in the day that you have really not thought through the actual underlying business characteristics. So the takeaway here for this Pocket NPV approach is to put hand to paper before you put hand to laptop.

For those interested, the tables below capture in numerical form the pictures we've drawn to date. The first table contains the NPV components for each of the three options. The second table calculates the Net Present Value of each option for four different scenarios of discount rate.

Components

Components ($m)	K	CF1	CF2	CF3	CF4	CF5	TV
Option A	2	0.5	0.5	0.5	0.5	0.5	5
Option B	12	0.0	0.7	1.5	1.5	1.5	15
Option C	5	-2.5	0.0	1.0	2.0	2.0	20

	Discount Rates (r)	5%	10%	15%	20%
NPV ($m)					
Option A		4.1	3.0	2.2	1.5
Option B		4.1	1.0	-1.4	-3.3
Option C		12.4	8.5	5.6	3.3

The first thing that jumps out at us here is that, if all three options are equally risky (i.e. same discount rate for all) then Option C is always the best option, and Option B is always the worst. A second takeaway from this Pocket NPV simulation is that for Option A to be a financially better option than Option C, its risk would have to be much lower. Only if Option C is so risky that we apply a discount rate of 20 per cent, and

Option A so safe that we apply a discount rate of 5 per cent, does Option A yield a higher NPV ($4.1 million versus $3.3 million). If Option C is moderately risky, we can conclude that it is the best of the three options on the table, with an NPV in the range of $5 million to $10 million.

The Pocket NPV process we've been through is quick, highly visual and light on data. It results in simple, clear numbers that underpin a financial assessment of multiple options. Where the Memorable Metrics of the Balanced Scorecard tell you what to obsess about to make your initiative or venture a success, the Pocket NPV gives you a rough size of the prize in case of success.

To link the two, one usually needs a whole batch of assumptions, and some kind of model. This is really hard to present in theory as a stand-alone, so instead let's use a simple illustration. We'll keep the same example-cum-exercise to link Memorable Metrics, basic model, and Pocket NPV.

Simple Numbers example

After homes, experiences and restaurants, let's pretend that Airbnb is now thinking of adding a fourth line of service: friends. Airbnb Friends would help people meet others at their destination, with similar tastes in culture, life, business, etc. What would the Memorable Metrics for success be for this, and what would a Pocket NPV look like for different versions of the service?

Why would Airbnb launch such a service, by the way? Perhaps as a new revenue stream if city authorities start clamping down on the provision of short-term rentals around the world. Or maybe getting any visitors to a city to use the 'Friends' function might also be a great pipeline for Airbnb's other existing services.

For example, Paris welcomes 40 million visitors every year, and Airbnb offers 50,000 listings there. Even if each listing were to welcome the enormous amount of 60 different visitors every year, Airbnb would still only account for 8 per cent of visitors to Paris. Getting visitors to use Airbnb Friends first (aka AirFriends, shortened to 'AF') might complement and feed into the core business quite well. A scorecard for the AirFriends initiative at inception might look as below.

Financial

- **Subscription** (£/visitor)
- **Tips** (£/hour/visitor)
- **Cost** (£/hour/ visitor)

Customer

- # AF **encounters**
- # AF encounters per **visitor**
- % positive **feedback**

AIRFRIENDS PARIS

Process

- # AF-using **visitors**
- # local AF **hosts**
- # encounter categories (arts, sports, etc)

Growth

- # weekly **encounters/host**
- **% bad** encounters
- # AF-friendly **venues**

Taking this one step further, we've modelled below how many local volunteers AirFriends would roughly need in Paris to meet the demands of potential users. There are a number of modelling variables for Airbnb's current business (how many visits a year an average Airbnb listing welcomes, how many visitors travel together on average, how many listings on average an individual host manages, etc.) and for the future demand for the AirFriends proposition (share of Airbnb visitors that will use AirFriends, how many times on each trip, etc.).

We've then looked at the supply side, and envisaged two stages: either the visitors only have encounters with Airbnb hosts, or they can also get to meet volunteers (who can be anyone in Paris).

The very rough simulation below makes two things quite clear. First, even with a low rate of enthusiasm by visitors (10 per cent using AirFriends, and only twice on any trip) the supply of possible encounters by Airbnb hosts falls well short of the demand, and AirFriends will have to rely on an external army of volunteers.

Second, as a very rough estimate, the number of volunteers required is probably in the order of magnitude of 5 per cent of the number of Airbnb listings in the area, suggesting 2,500+ volunteers in Paris alone. This simple model implies that AirFriends would need a serious effort at recruiting volunteers to succeed.

AIRFRIENDS IN PARIS	DEMAND	SUPPLY 1 With Airbnb hosts	SUPPLY 2 With AirFriends volunteers
Total Airbnb listings	50,000		
Average Airbnb trips/Airbnb listing	30		
Average Airbnb visitors/trip	2.0		
Total Airbnb visitors	3,000,000		
% of Airbnb visitors using AirFriends	10%		
Average encounters / AirFriend user	2		
Total AirFriends encounters sought by visitors	600,000		
Average Airbnb listings / Airbnb host		1.25	
% of Airbnb hosts offering AirFriends		10%	
Total Airbnb hosts on AirFriends		4,000	
Encounter offered / week / host		0.5	
Average weeks / year / host		25.0	
Encounter offered / host		12.5	
Total AirFriends encounters offered by hosts		50,000	
Total AirFriends encounters offered by volunteers			550,000
Average encounters offered / week / volunteer			5
Average weeks / year / volunteer			44
Total number of AirFriends volunteers			2,500
Ratio of AirFriends volunteers to Airbnb listings			5%

Simple Numbers exercise: How to make friends with Airbnb?

Now that you are familiar with our imaginary AirFriends proposition, let's construct a Pocket NPV around a few options for execution.

To keep things simple, imagine that you are the founder and CEO of AirFriends, and that it has nothing to do with Airbnb. It is just a stand-alone business, connecting local volunteers with visiting tourists and business people, to organize short cultural encounters. Once up and running, AirFriends could strike partnerships with many platforms (Airbnb, Facebook, LinkedIn, Bumble, etc.) to make its services available to their members. Let's envisage three options:

> **Option A: Language for Tips.** Locals who want to practise a foreign language (language students, aspiring tour guides, etc.) meet for drinks or a meal with foreign visitors, and make recommendations on lesser-known local cultural gems (La Butte aux Cailles neighbourhood rather than Le Marais, etc.).

> **Option B: Business Networking.** Local professionals from a given industry (consulting, advertising, aeronautics, etc.) meet with foreign visitors from the same industry. Building international business contacts via serendipity.

> **Option C: Twins for Life.** Meet people who are the local version of you. Whatever your age, gender, profession, etc. as a visitor, at least a couple of the many volunteers in Paris will be spookily similar to you in background, cultural tastes, etc. Meeting them could open the door to friendships for life.

You can choose to compare the financial aspects of these three options via a complex Excel model, or a simpler Pocket NPV. Either way, feel free to share your solution on www.strategic.how/numbers and we'll gladly offer feedback.

10.

COMPELLING STORY

Using the Pyramid Principle at the end of projects

We've seen in the 'Pyramid Principle' chapter that Barbara Minto has unearthed a storytelling gem. When it comes to telling a compelling story at the end of a project, the Pyramid is the best structure there is.

Remember that the pyramidal approach can be used at both ends of any project: at the beginning, to create Clarity from chaos, and now at the end, to support your recommendation with Conviction.

One big difference between applying the Pyramid Principle at the end of a project, compared to at the beginning of a project, is the absence of the word 'if' before every Post-it. There are no ifs at the end of a project. We have the data and we can assert things. By comparison, there are lots of ifs at the beginning of a project. We don't have any data, and the only thing we can do is structure the chaos, through hypothetical conjecture. If 'A turns out true' and if 'B turns out true', and if 'C turns out true', then 'D', the Post-it on the level above, will turn out true as a result.

MINTO'S RULES FOR USING THE PYRAMID PRINCIPLE AT THE END OF PROJECTS

Barbara Minto offers five rules to ensure you present with Conviction at the end of a project, and we'll go over each in turn.

1. Structure your ideas in a **pyramid form**
2. Present your ideas from the **top down**
3. Have your ideas in the pyramid obey three sub-rules
   a. Ideas at each level are **summaries** of the ideas grouped below

    b. Ideas in each grouping are part of an **inductive or deduct-ive** argument

    c. Ideas in each grouping are in a **logical** order

4. Make sure the **vertical** relationships work

5. Make sure the **horizontal** relationships work

Each tip will become second nature to you over time. In the meantime, let's go into further depth on each.

1. Structure your ideas in a pyramid form

This means fit your presentation into a shape that looks like a pyramid, typically putting two or three building blocks below each building block, and continuing downwards. Hence the name of the technique. One big building block at the top, three blocks in the next level down, nine under that, 27 for the next level, 81, 243, etc. Projects and presentations rarely get to 243 components, but you get the gist. Everywhere in your presentations you create mini-pyramids of building blocks (one above, two or three below). Sticky notes are the best support for this, and I usually refer to these building blocks as 'Post-its'.

2. Present your ideas from the top down

Remember that we are now at the point of Conviction, and we know the answer to the project, so we can be quite crisp and assertive. Imagine as an example that we've been asked by the Greek agora to find out if Socrates is mortal. At the end of the project, once we know the answer for sure, the best way to present is to start from the top indeed, and state clearly: 'Socrates is mortal'. Details can come later, to support this main contention.

3. Ideas in the pyramid have to obey three sub-rules

The first sub-rule is that 'ideas at each level are summaries of the ideas grouped below'. We split our big statement into smaller ones that support it. In our example, you can see that we've added 'Men are mortal', and 'Socrates is a man' below our main conclusion that 'Socrates is mortal'. The idea at the top is clearly a summary of the ideas grouped below.

The second sub-rule is that 'ideas in each grouping are part of an inductive or deductive argument'. Our example with Socrates is a mini-pyramid built on a deductive argument.

Deductive

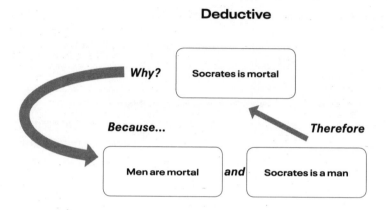

The top contention, 'Socrates is mortal', is arrived at by deducing the answer from the ideas in the level below. *Because* 'Men are mortal', *and* 'Socrates is a man', *therefore* 'Socrates is mortal'. We need to be at the end of the project, with facts at hand, to be able to state the component building blocks in that way. We now know that men are mortal (because, for example, we visited a morgue), and we now know that Socrates is a man (because, for example, a member of our team interviewed two members of his gym). This combination of facts allows us to deduce our answer above, that 'Socrates is mortal'.

Let's now examine a mini-pyramid using an inductive argument, by looking at the contention that 'India is a great place for global businesses to come to'. How can we break that overall statement into components from which we can induce the positive answer we seek?

We can write the following three Post-its: 'Japanese businesses invest successfully in India', 'German businesses invest successfully in India', and 'US and other businesses invest successfully in India'. Once we get the data on these three statements, and it comes back positive, we'll be able to conclude, via induction, that indeed 'India is a great place for global businesses to come to'.

You will have noticed that the inductive logic feels looser than the deductive logic. There's a bit more room for disagreement.

Inductive

The reason we have both logics to choose from is that sometimes deductive logic is not available for a given issue.

The third sub-rule is 'ideas in each grouping must be in a logical order'. This is a little bit more subjective. It's about storytelling. In our inductive example, if you present to a Japanese audience you might start with 'Japanese businesses invest successfully in India', whereas you might swap the first two Post-its if you present to a German audience. The logical order in each horizontal grouping is one where you start with the (subjectively) most important Post-it on the left, and then position the other two to the right to tell the story in a way that makes the most sense for the audience. What's not subjective is the fourth rule.

4. Make sure the vertical relationships work

How do you do that? We've seen it already in the two mini-pyramid examples above. You use the words 'why', 'because', 'and', 'therefore'. You create a triangular shape. 'Socrates is mortal'. **Why** is he mortal? **Because** 'men are mortal' **and** 'Socrates is a man', **therefore** 'Socrates is mortal'. These four words – why, because, and, therefore – make the vertical relationship between the levels.

5. Make sure the horizontal relationships work

How do you do that? In a deductive argument, the second point has to comment on the first one. 'Socrates is a man', 'men are mortal' . . . 'men' comments on 'man', so that works. In an inductive argument, it's about making sure that you can summarize all the components as a plural. 'Businesses from *lots of different countries* invest successfully in India', so that works too.

In summary

We've now covered the five simple rules you need to follow to apply the Pyramid Principle at the point of Conviction, at the end of projects. Of course, you can front-load some of these rules and start applying them early in the project too. For example, when creating a whole new level under a Post-it, it might help to try both the deductive and the inductive logic approach to discover the best way to structure that issue. Following the rules early on is useful, following them at the end is essential for your story to prove compelling.

Examples of Pyramids used throughout projects

You'll see below the structure for our Harley-Davidson example, used both at the beginning and at the end of the project. You will notice that the only difference is the two big words around the structure. 'If' and 'then' are used at the beginning. Should the data support it, the big words at the end of the project become 'because' and 'therefore'. 'If' and 'then' make a story credible. 'Because' and 'therefore' make a story compelling.

Sometimes the data gathered over the course of the project doesn't support a specific component of the pyramid. For example, let's say we wrote early in the Harley-Davidson project a Post-it with 'it [the European apparel market] is growing at a good rate'. (NB: this is the second Post-it from the left in the bottom row of the pyramid). What if we find out that the market growth rate is actually flat? The fact we eventually gather disagrees with our initial Post-it, but it doesn't invalidate our logic. With this fact in hand, we can now change our initial Post-it of the market growing at a 'good rate' into 'a very slow rate'. This changes the Post-it above from the market being 'very attractive' into 'somewhat attractive', and the top recommendation goes from enter the market 'in a big way' to enter 'cautiously'.

AT THE BEGINNING OF THE PROJECT

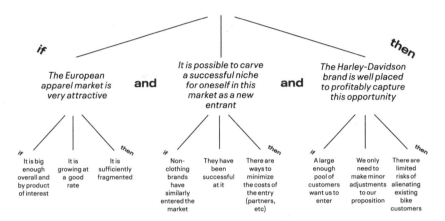

AT THE END OF THE PROJECT

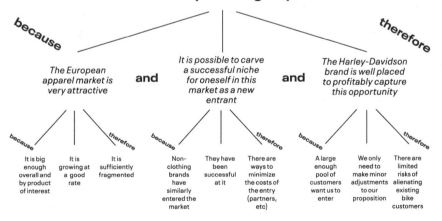

You will notice in the picture below that we only need to change a few words (in the black boxes) to adjust the pre-existing structure to the new reality. The final recommendation changes because of the facts, but the structure of the presentation stays the same.

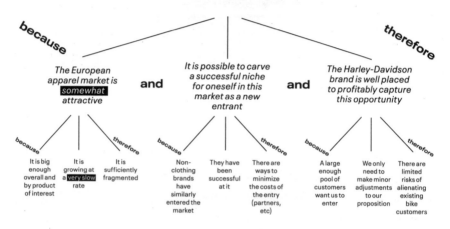

A strategic thinker is able to use the Pyramid Principle throughout any project. First by building an early version with the most desirable outcome at the top of the page (as we saw in detail in the 'Pyramid Principle' chapter). Then by adjusting the words in the structure as the data comes in. And finally, by using the rules to present convincingly at the end when an actual project conclusion and recommendation have emerged.

A good pyramid is like a Swiss army knife: the perfect companion tool to a versatile travel adventure. Let's look at a journey towards musical success. Let's pretend a music major, Universal, Warner, or Sony BMG, wants to secure the number one spot in the music charts at Christmas in your home country.

As you can imagine, many businesses in hit-driven industries (film, fashion, music, pharmaceuticals, publishing, etc.) always strive for the hits. The Pyramid Principle is a great way to structure early in the project what it would take to secure that hit in due course. You'll definitely gain a much better idea, level by level, of all the tasks, resources and processes required to achieve the outcome that you seek.

"Universal tops the music charts at Christmas this year"

Our single is the best **product**	and	We have the most effective **marketing**	and	We have the widest **distribution**

The **song** is highly catchy and totally right for Christmas	The **artist** already has a huge following	The **video** is uniquely compelling and viral	We have blanketed the **social media** world, with a 'hook' for viral speed	We have many **affiliates** to cross promote with (charities, guest singers, etc)	There are attention-grabbing **events** lined up to feed the social and affiliate engines	We have a privileged position on all the **digital platforms** that matter	Our **physical supply chain** is totally spike-proof	The single can be easily **gifted** in multiple quirky ways

The possible solution above was put together by four people with no professional experience of the music industry at all, in 45 minutes, at one of my live training sessions. It looks pretty convincing, either at the beginning of the project (to try and achieve the hit) or at the end of the project (to explain why and how the hit was achieved). Please note the pyramid doesn't guarantee a hit at Christmas. It does, however, offer a great structure to ask for investments (in social media, video, physical distribution, etc.), and to explain how you will achieve the outcome you seek.

The Universal exercise shouldn't be too difficult for anybody with a passing interest in music. Why don't you have a go at another structure in a few weeks' time (without rereading the paragraphs above!). If you work in another hit-driven industry, ask yourself how you would achieve a number one hit in your industry. Maybe number one video game, number one app, number one consulting product, etc. See if you can borrow this pyramid and customize it to tell your compelling story.

Adland Swagger

Strategic issues come in many varied shapes and sizes. The only traits they share are a focus on the future, and data that is often both scarce and unreliable. Convincing a third party to back your conclusions in this context is no mean feat.

We've seen so far the importance of impactful words (NLP Language, 10 Ways to Convince), of simple numbers (Memorable Metrics, Pocket NPV), and of a good storytelling structure (Pyramid Principle). The last ingredient needed to tie this all together is a bit of Adland Swagger.

Adland is a shorthand term for the advertising industry and all its components. The marketing directors wanting to increase the exposure of a given product, the creative agencies producing great ads with stunning visuals and witty copy, the media agencies buying airtime and space on multiple channels for the ads to reach their intended audience, etc.

The business of adland is conviction. All adland does is convince people to agree with a message, usually quickly, sometimes repeatedly. They have extracted a few simple rules for success that we can borrow. Grabbing a teenager's attention on Instagram in two seconds is not the same as convincing an entirely middle-aged board of directors at your company over several hours or months, but a few techniques overlap.

Allow me to share here the three I've found the most effective over time.

THREE-WORD SUMMARY

An idea summarized in three words is highly portable. Your colleagues, customers or bosses don't need access to the full underlying business case to spread the word. They can just repeat the three words. You will remember from the section on NLP that this will work particularly well for people with strong auditory or kinaesthetic preference (as three-word summaries can be shared by word of mouth during watercooler moments with other people – be it around a physical watercooler or the digital equivalents that are Slack, Microsoft Teams, WhatsApp, etc.).

Many industries have codified the three-word summary as a way to talk about new ideas or existing propositions. Adland loves a good three-word slogan. 'Just do It' (Nike), 'Finger lickin' good' (KFC), 'World's favourite airline' (British Airways), etc. Venture capitalists and the tech world often use the three-word summary as a shorthand for new ventures 'Uber for dogwalking', 'Airbnb for parking spaces', 'Meds on tap', etc. This makes it easy to remember the full-size deck or the presentation. The film industry can similarly often capture the essence of a film in development in a very crisp description. Sometimes the crisp summary makes it all the way into the film title, as with 'Snakes on a plane' or 'Hobo with a gun'. In whatever context, the three- (or four-) word summary is an exercise in extracting the essence of what you're presenting to others, and making it all the more memorable.

ONE SIMPLE VISUAL

A picture is worth a thousand words. We all know it, even before realizing that over a third of people have a strong visual preference, meaning the expression is actually very true for them.

At the intersection of business and academia, new concepts travel all the better and that much further when they are accompanied by a simple visual. Porter's Five Forces below meet that criterion, and (hopefully) so too does the Rollercoaster of Strategic Thinking.

A recent client of mine wanted to convince several thousand employees of the value of putting customers at the heart of everything they did. Walking the walk of customer-centricity, not just talking the talk. The CEO had a brilliant, extensive and well-argued presentation that she took to all corners of the organization. It explained the rationale for the shift, highlighted new procedures, and modelled the benefits that would ensue for everyone. She also ended each talk with the third image below. Crisp, clear and memorable. Worth a thousand words.

Porter's 5 Forces

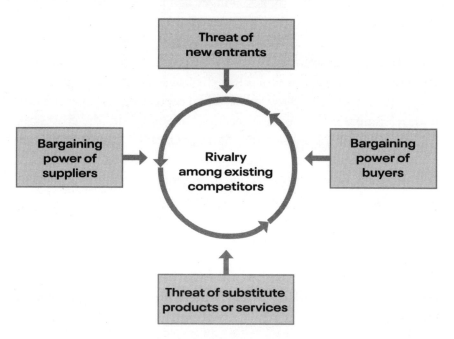

Rollercoaster
of Strategic Thinking

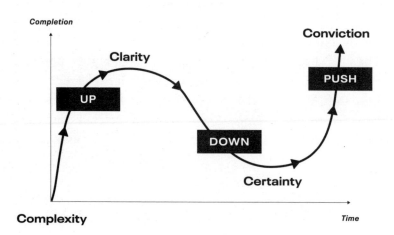

Product
centric

Customer
centric

TWO HUMAN ANECDOTES

Business documents can get dry very quickly. Excel spreadsheets, legal disclaimers, management speak. It's easy to lose sight of the fact that you, a human being, are trying to convince other human beings to back you, and to take on board the recommendations your team have crafted. Introducing a couple of human anecdotes into the proceedings goes a long way towards making your story more compelling.

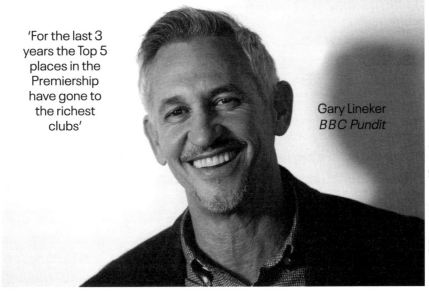

'For the last 3 years the Top 5 places in the Premiership have gone to the richest clubs'

Gary Lineker
BBC Pundit

Image © Dave J. Hogan/Getty Images

Imagine that you're helping an investor buy a share of a football club in the UK, and they're wondering about the relationship between turnover and success in the Premiership. You will naturally gather a fair amount of historical data, analyse it extensively, and probably display a trendline on a smart scatter plot. A simple quote from beloved pundit Gary Lineker won't have the same quantitative truth as your analysis, but it will add a compelling qualitative impact, a human touch.

In many business contexts, this human touch is best provided by customers, employees or competitors, rather than celebrities. Picking a couple of representative individuals is a great way to give a human face to your analysis and recommendation. Selecting just one individual is a bit risky. There might be specific issues you may not be aware of that might invalidate their perceived representativeness. Conversely, three people might create too much variety in the views expressed, thereby diluting your message. Two's the charm.

IN SUMMARY

My own summary for what we've just seen is: **1 visual, 2 people, 3 words.**

Finally, Adland Swagger wouldn't be complete if we didn't mention music, colour, repetition, etc. There are many techniques used by advertising specialists to engage our attention and obtain our approval. These are beyond the scope of this book, but I invite you to explore for yourself, by browsing through the opus of David Ogilvy, John Hegarty or Seth Godin.

Compelling Story exercise:
How to make your organization strategic?

Imagine that you have been tasked with making your organization more strategic. For the sake of this exercise, your organization might mean a team of 10 people, a startup of 100 colleagues, a consulting firm of 1,000 consultants, an NGO with 10,000 volunteers, or a multinational company with 100,000+ employees.

The time frame you have been given to deliver a recommendation will vary depending on the size and professionalism of this organization, from a few days to a few months. What won't change is that you'll have four ways available to you to solve the problem: the expert, analytical, creative and strategic ways.

The expert way would probably involve you inviting a few external experts to pitch, selecting one based on credentials and methodology, and asking her to plot a path forward. The analytical way might involve benchmarking comparable organizations, interviewing internal stakeholders, etc. and analysing all that data to slowly and carefully produce a considered recommended solution over time. The creative way would likely see you bring a few people together, quickly generating several possible avenues to make your organization more strategic, and then letting people mull over each option, to ultimately choose the approach they like best, based on taste, personal preferences and emerging consensus.

Finally, there is the strategic way: the Rollercoaster approach I would suggest here. Starting with an 'Up' drive, quickly generating a range of options, and then a 'Down' leg, exposing these options to the harsh reality of data (words, numbers, actions), before finally packaging your recommended solution with a good 'Push'.

In some organizations you might end up producing a 50-page PowerPoint deck to support your case, while in others a three-word slogan might be the preferred delivery mode. If you look back to Apple public presentations over the years (by Steve Jobs and Tim Cook), you will notice that their favourite house style for convincing an audience is a few simple slides, with one big photo and one big number on each. At Amazon, meanwhile, the recommended approach is a six-page narrative memo. A good halfway house might be a combination of three slides, as illustrated below: a one-page executive summary (mostly words-based), one metrics scorecard (mostly numbers-based), and one pyramid to 27 Post-its (mostly story-based).

Do share your version of the answer to this exercise on www.strategic.how/story and we'll gladly offer feedback. Feel free to use as much NLP, 10 Ways to Convince, Pocket NPV, Memorable Metrics and Adland Swagger as you like!

COMPELLING STORY EXERCISE:
THREE SLIDES

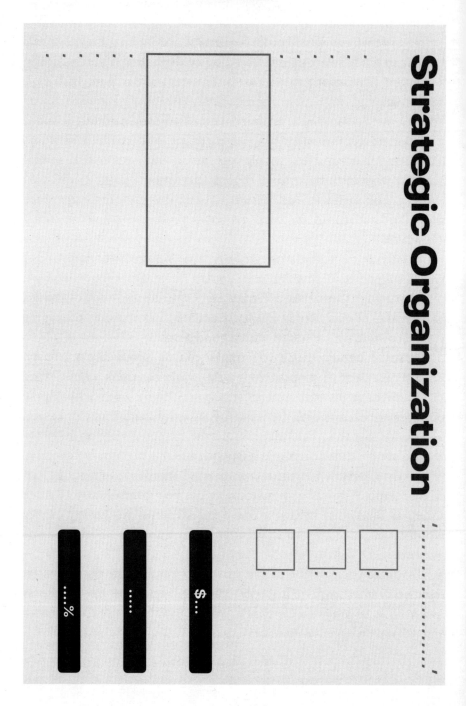

Strategic Organization

Strategic Organization

Financial

- ....
- ....
- ....

Customer

- ....
- ....
- ....

STRATEGIC ORGANIZATION

Process

- ....
- ....
- ....

Growth

- ....
- ....
- ....

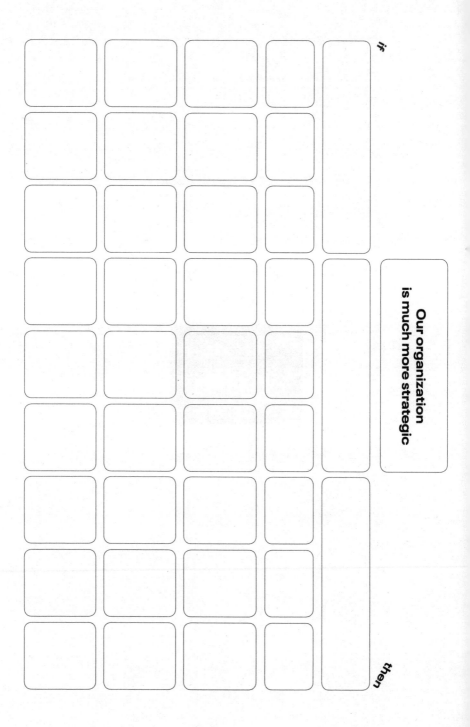

Our organization
is much more strategic

if

then

PART FIVE

HOW TO KEEP IMPROVING AS A STRATEGIC THINKER ('AGAIN')

We're coming to the end of the book. Whether you've read every chapter or not yet, you are now in possession of a new insight, a new mindset and a wide toolset.

The **insight** is that there are four ways to solve problems, and the strategic way is the most important, and the least well practised. The new **mindset** is that solving strategic issues requires you to ride the Rollercoaster of Strategic Thinking, through the three phases of 'Up', 'Down' and 'Push'. The wide **toolset** is comprised of a number of techniques for each phase in the rollercoaster: Pyramid Principle, Happy Line and Mutation Game for 'Up'; Payoff Profiles, Landscape Analysis and Lean Startup for 'Down'; NLP Language, Memorable Metrics, Adland Swagger, etc. for 'Push'.

Once you put the book down, it is time to apply this in practice. In your life and at work. Here are five suggestions for you, to make sure the learning sticks.

> **Do the exercises in each chapter.** It's easy to read a book from cover to cover and ignore the exercises. As you're near the end, now is a good moment to retrace your steps and actually take the time to do the exercises, to embed the learning.

> **Find a 'buddy' to practise with.** Every study into the efficiency of learning new skills highlights the importance of a fellow peer to learn with. Give someone you respect a copy of this book, and commit to reviewing each other's solutions to the exercises, comparing techniques used, etc.

> **Read more.** From Bill Gates down, a lot of very senior and

successful executives underline the importance of reading smart, thoughtful business books. Not necessarily every day, but at least once in a while. Make sure you always have at least one such book opened at your desk.

> **Mull over the five tips in the next chapter.** These five key tips for more strategic thinking were an attempt at creating a modern Jenga puzzle for you. I started with a big pile of 30 pieces of advice and removed the least useful ones, one after the other, to be left with the absolutely essential ones.

> **Get ready for the advanced techniques.** This book is laser-focused on giving you a dozen techniques on 'How to Be Strategic'. You will see results very quickly when you start applying them in your life and your job. When the stakes get higher, you'll need techniques for high-altitude problem solving. Google can help you there, as can the *Harvard Business Review*, and you'll also find a few more useful resources on this book's website.

Becoming fluent in the strategic way to solve problems is very much like learning a new language. The previous chapters have given you some grammar and quite a bit of new vocabulary. This final chapter is a guided tour through some key aspects of the culture of people who use strategic thinking every day.

11

FIVE KEY TIPS FOR MORE STRATEGIC THINKING

Tip 1: The third solution is often the best

Why is the first idea that comes to mind usually not the best? I don't know why. All I can say is that when looking back at the path taken to get to the ultimate solution on projects over the years, I've often noticed that the first couple of answers or options were rarely the ones that made it. Maybe you have noticed this too?

However, this only applies when the issue at stake is strategic. On problems where expertise can be brought to bear, the expert's first option is usually pretty good. That is the definition of expertise! If the problem is slightly more complicated, and two experts bring two different angles or options to the debate, they might agree on a middle ground, aka a third solution. So why is it that the more complex the issue, the more likely it is that the early options are not as good as the later ones?

We saw earlier, in the 'NLP Language' section, how different preferences in representation channel can affect people's ability to process information. Another insight from NLP is that the internal dialogue we all have with our own selves can also affect our ability to solve problems.

Imagine that you're looking for a solution, and have just found one. Your internal voice could speak to you on a continuum from A) 'Well done, you're a star, call it a day', to B) 'That's a good start, what else is there out there?', or even to C) 'That's probably not the answer, it's too hard for you, and you won't find anything else.'

This internal dialogue is not that different from having a coach inside your mind, or a set of angels and demons sitting on your shoulders. Coach A is highly supportive, coach B less so, and coach C is very critical. From a problem-solving point of view, both extremes, A and C, are sub-optimal. Though completely different in their intentions (strong praise versus strong criticism), both approaches will likely lead you to stop the search for more options. Out of satisfaction or dejection. Coach B, on the other hand, gives you credit for the effort carried out to date, and inserts a tiny bit of tension to motivate you to keep on searching.

However unconscious this internal dialogue might feel, one of the now widely adopted discoveries of NLP is the realization that each one of us actually has control over it. Cognitive Behavioural Therapy, the most successful form of therapy of the last 30 years, rests on very little more than exactly that. Slightly changing the words one uses with oneself, in order to slightly change the emotions one experiences as a result, and leading to slightly changed behaviours that improve one's emotions, etc. This feedback loop is typically used very productively with people suffering from body image issues, addictions, anxiety, depression, etc. Problem-solving anxiety is a very simple issue in comparison, and changing the internal dialogue one uses with oneself to achieve more positive outcomes is all the more successful. It doesn't guarantee you a solution, but it's a good start.

When it comes to enhancing your strategic problem-solving skills on the spot, a good sentence to use in your internal dialogue is: 'What are two widely different solutions to this problem?'

Asking yourself 'Are there two different solutions to this problem?' might make you hesitate, wonder, answer 'I don't know', etc. Teeing up your brain instead with 'What are two widely different solutions to this problem?' treats the strategic issue you face as a riddle you can solve, rather than a big black hole. It starts from the premise that there are two such options out there, and these just need to be discovered. Like an Easter egg hunt. Once you come across the first option, your internal dialogue isn't going to claim victory; just celebrate the discovery of the first egg, and keep on looking for more.

Once that is done, the next sentence to turn to is to tell yourself: 'The third solution is often the best.' Why? First, because this will re-energize you and your brain, prompting you to do a bit more work, and find a third great solution. Second, because your years of professional experience might have shown you how many winning solutions turned out to be the middle ground between two extreme options that were on the table earlier. Hence, the third solution is often the best.

Finally, there's another more powerful reason for telling yourself: 'The third solution is often the best.' By the time you have three options on the table, I can't guarantee that the third is actually the best. What I can guarantee, though, is that by then you are completely alert to the fact that options are everywhere around us. If so, what are the odds that there is a fourth great idea lying around waiting to be discovered? Quite good. And it's worth looking for it a little longer.

It takes time for most people to accept the reality that the first few options they'll think of on any complex issue are likely not the best. Once that sinks in, however, it becomes blindingly obvious that the best way to start solving a complex problem is by going 'Up' quickly, to get to Clarity and three or four early options.

In summary: the third solution is often the best. Even when that's not true, getting to a third solution quickly will massively increase your chances of solving the problem.

Tip 2: Small teams go 'Up', large teams go 'Down'

A classic conundrum when it comes to solving strategic problems in any organization is: 'How many people should we invite to help tackle issue X?' Sub-set questions include who exactly should we invite, and how should we run the meetings (as plenary sessions around one large table, as several small teams in breakout setup, etc.). In a nutshell: how many, who, and what setup?

Before answering that, I'd like to add a fourth dimension: temperament. Broadly speaking, there are three main problem-solving temperaments, whether you look at it from your own circle of friends and colleagues, or you borrow from the characters of A. A. Milne: Tigger, Eeyore, and Winnie-the-Pooh. Our personalities often determine how we approach new problems, and you can usually guess how different team members will contribute to the problem-solving effort in due course, depending on whether they are real-life Tiggers, Eeyores or Poohs.

Tigger's predominant personality trait is his bounciness. Tigger is hyperactive and fun-loving. He's not afraid of failure, and doesn't mind trying new things. If it doesn't work out, he will merrily bounce on to a new adventure. In Tigger's words, 'That's what Tiggers do best. Hoo hoo hoo hoo!' Tiggers are never happier, nor more useful, than in the 'Up' swing of problem solving, or in the 'Push' at the end.

Eeyore, on the other hand, is perpetually depressed. His cup is always half empty and he will always spot the dark cloud instead of the silver lining. That said, Eeyore is cautious and not at all gullible. He will never fall for half-baked new ideas. Why? Because he doesn't think anything good ever happens. Eeyore can drag teams down with his downbeat personality – but also spot flaws in new ideas. Eeyores are crucial to a good 'Down' swing of problem solving.

Finally, Winnie-the-Pooh is stable, lovable and loving. He tries to think the best of others, and keeps things on track. Pooh rolls with the punches, and he likes a well-balanced life. He is respected and well liked by all. Poohs are great team players who can ensure that the process is even-keeled, and who lend a hand throughout all three phases of any project ('Up', 'Down' and 'Push').

With this in mind, my suggestions for any strategic problem-solving activity is to make sure there are at least a third of Tiggers in the task-force, and preferably a third of each personality type. Tiggers are good for giving the impulse, Eeyores for spotting the flaws, and Poohs for keeping things ticking over.

How many people in total? It depends. Most taskforces or meetings include representatives from different strands in the company – be they functional specialists (strategy, marketing, finance, sales, etc.), territories (home market, established markets, new markets, etc.) or any other split. That usually ramps up the body count quite quickly. Which is not necessarily an issue in the 'Down' phase of problem solving. The more people around the table, the quicker the flaws in an idea will be spotted. From experience, meetings with between 12 and 16 people offer the sweet spot of broad expertise and personal involvement. Anything above that and people don't feel as committed – possibly because their turn to speak or contribute comes that much more infrequently. In a startup environment (or in startup mode in a larger organization) one could probably get a multitude of points of view with as few as four to six contributors.

You will have noticed that the three techniques seen in the 'Up' section of this book take one hour each to complete, and require at least four people. Small teams make it easier to achieve lift-off; because small teams pay attention to each participant's contribution – as there might be uncomfortable silence otherwise. Small teams go faster. In a larger meeting, instead, every time someone contributes a germ of an idea, there will always be at least one person ready to shoot it down right away.

Every problem is different, and every company is different. With these caveats in mind, the approach that seems to deliver the best outcome is something along these lines:

> a task force is assembled, of 12 to 16 people
> two meetings are held, one hour each, a few weeks apart
> a memo describing the problem is circulated to all by the issue owner before the first meeting. Not too much data, and half a page max
> the first meeting focuses on an 'Up' session. The participants are split into three or four small teams of four or five people each. Randomly mixing functions and seniority, but ensuring at least one Tigger per team
> small teams start work in parallel (using the same technique) and swap over after 15–20 minutes, to get a new diagnostic and to generate new ideas
> each participant votes on their three favourite ideas (excluding their own)
> a memo capturing the five to 10 best ideas overall is circulated by the issue owner. A few lines per idea, with a catchy name and a sense of the upside
> the second meeting focuses on a 'Down' session. Conducted as a plenary session, ensuring that all objections are captured and acted upon right away
> the issue owner tasks three specific sub-groups within the taskforce with progressing the final three best ideas after the meeting, one idea per sub-group.

In summary: use small teams to go 'Up', and large teams to go 'Down'.

Tip 3: The Post-it is mightier than the pen

Imagine that you're running a meeting or a workshop, designed to crack a complex strategic issue – for your team, your function, your division, your whole company, etc. You've invited 12 to 16 people, and they are already arranged in smaller teams for the 'Up' exercise(s). What do you do next? Get people to stand up.

Most people have working habits that physically don't help during the 'Up' swing of strategic problem solving. Indeed, most people spend their days working alone, sitting down, at their laptop, and often in silence. As you become more senior, you still find yourself sitting down for most of the time, but instead of working alone in silence you might spend your days in meetings, listening to other people – and waiting for your turn to speak. I simplify drastically but this is not far off reality.

Sitting-down desktop work is quite good for linear, productive output, and sitting-down meetings can be quite good for collaborative decision making. What both these approaches are not good for is right-brain, intuitive and creative idea generation. Nor for left-brain, structured and planned idea generation either.

Firstly, most creative endeavour notoriously comes from a different body position: slouching or standing up, not sitting down. Many a great song was started with a musician nonchalantly strumming a few chords on their guitar while slouching across a sofa during a late-night session of merriment. Likewise, many a creative blockage has been unpicked by a walk in the park, a run or a shower.

On the latter, Oscar-winning screenwriter Aaron Sorkin takes up to eight showers a day. The author of *West Wing*, *The Social Network* and *The Newsroom* has installed a small shower unit in his office to keep his creativity flowing, after realizing that he often got his best ideas in the shower. He says, 'I take six to eight showers a day. I'm not a germaphobe, it's not like that. I find them incredibly refreshing and when writing isn't going well, it's a do over . . . I will shower, change into new clothes and start again.'

Most of us don't have the luxury of installing a shower unit in our office, but we can draw inspiration from one insight: a lot of new ideas come to us when standing up. The other insight should be that no idea ever comes to us in a fully formed fashion. After the first flash of inspiration, the contribution needs to be revised, altered and polished, again and again.

Pretend you have just arrived at a first draft of a pyramid exercise, as below. You are the project leader, and a team member has just suggested something that will alter the structure. What do you do next? Your reaction is likely to be a function of both the quality of the suggestion, and of the physical support of your current draft.

Imagine that there are three versions of the mini-pyramid below: one written with pen on paper (Paper), one written with erasable marker pens on whiteboard (Board), and one with Post-its stuck on a window or a wall (Post-its).

Changing the Post-its version is physically straightforward, and therefore there is a really low quality threshold to embracing new team suggestions. Any suggestion, however marginal, that strikes you and the team as an improvement to the current draft output will be welcomed. Writing a new Post-it with the suggestion on it, moving a few other Post-its around, *et voilà* – a new draft in 10 seconds.

In the case of the two other physical supports (Paper, Board), altering the current draft has a higher price. Ugly scratch marks on a pristine draft (Paper), or having to wipe away and rewrite whole sections to make way for the new comment (Board). I have seen countless times how a facilitator will push back against the same marginal comment if the physical support is painful to alter – creating a higher threshold for embracing team suggestions, and disappointing contributors more for the same level of contribution. The same issue applies irrespective of the technique used (Happy Line, Mutation Game, Payoff Profiles, etc.). The choice of physical support on which the team captures its work-in-progress has an impact on the team dynamics and the ultimate quality of the final product. And so does the choice of body positions.

In summary: the Post-it is mightier than the pen – all the more so when used with everyone standing up!

Tip 4: Vote first, then debate

The yin and yang of strategic thinking are divergent thinking and convergent thinking. Breathing out and breathing in.

> **Divergent thinking** relishes differences, invites complexity, encourages different options, and splits hairs to create ever more numerous variants of anything.
> **Convergent thinking** tries to get to one outcome quickly, is productivity minded, decisive, conscious of time elapsing and budget running out.

In my experience, the classic meeting setup aims for convergent thinking but ends up in unsatisfactory divergent territory. For one simple reason: discussing different points of view inherently creates divergence. Left unattended, two people with broadly similar views could end up discussing the same issue for five minutes at a time, simply because of tiny differences in their views. One needs to proactively manage the meeting's process to allow it to breathe in and out. Diverging and converging several times in succession over the course of an hour. Every stage in the Rollercoaster of Strategic Thinking contains multiple instances of both.

In a Happy Line exercise, for example, the thinking starts divergent, with each participant coming up with a key purchasing criterion (KPC) that the other participants haven't thought of yet. Adding to the group's output by diverging from the current path. Most organizations are good at that. The notion that a team member contributes fully by adding new opinions to an existing problem is completely accepted – and even welcomed. Then, once there are 12 or more KPCs on the flipchart, one member in the team will usually remark that this might be enough, and that the team now needs to rank the criteria in decreasing order of importance. Choosing the top three criteria from a list of 12 is a classic piece of convergent thinking. Here, many organizations follow one of two sub-optimal approaches.

In some organizations, the HiPPO principle we saw earlier (Highest Paid Person's Opinion) is in full swing, and the convergence takes 10 seconds. The HiPPO chooses, and the others assent. The downside here, of course, is missing out on the input from all the other participants, and relying on the first answer as the best. In other, more modern, organizations, the selection of three criteria from 12 is treated as a fully collaborative exercise, where everyone contributes and weighs in. Great in principle, often sub-optimal in practice. Because people who have tiny differences of opinion can still spend hours debating them at great length. (I have frequently seen a team of five people held back for minutes at a time by two teammates who disagree on the order between the second and the third KPCs.)

What is one to do, to find the right mix of convergent thinking and collaborative work? There are three elements to factor in:

> how important is the issue being debated?
> how material is the impact of the difference between the options?
> is there a better approach to converge faster without so much debating?

On the importance of the issue being debated, it is always worth remembering the 'Bike-shedding' syndrome. The term 'Bike-shedding' comes from an apocryphal committee that had to approve the plans for a nuclear power station and for a bike shed. Knowing little about nuclear power stations, they talk about it briefly and just approve the recommendation put in front of them. Since they all know about bike sheds, they talk about it for hours, arguing about construction methods and paint choice and everything. 'Bike-shedding' is a memorable expression for alerting a group of people to the fact that they might be focusing on irrelevant matters.

On the impact of the different options, things are quite simple. Either the two options create two different outcomes, or they don't. If the outcome is the same under either option, then let's stop arguing and pick one (with a flick of a coin if need be). If, however, the two options create different outcomes, then let's pick both and deal with each in turn. So ask yourself first what the difference in outcome is, before deciding how many of the two options you need to carry forward.

Finally, on the issue of the technique, I use a lot of colourful dots in my training. Once the team has finished the divergent phase of an activity, I give each participant a batch of colourful sticky dots. Each person sticks the dots on their preferred choice, in 10 seconds, in silence. The specifics vary depending on the technique being used (Happy Line, Pyramid Principle, Mutation Game, etc.), but the results are always the same: much faster convergence, with less acrimony.

You will be amazed at how quick and painless this process is. Vote first, then debate. The dots allow each participant to feel that their opinion matters, and that it has been heard. In 10 seconds for all, not one minute each. It also helps participants spot where the majority view in the team is going, and whether they believe strongly enough in the importance of their small disagreement with the consensus to stand up to it and debate. This dots-based process doesn't eliminate debate, it prioritizes it. Don't waste time discussing things everyone broadly agrees on. Makes sure that the time spent debating is channelled towards the issues that matter the most, and where the difference between the options is material.

In summary: in convergent thinking, vote first, then debate. Not the other way round. The dots have it (as the Westminster Parliament's Speaker would say).

Tip 5: Say hi to AI

Artificial Intelligence is the biggest revolution yet to happen to complex business problem solving. The increasing prevalence of digital technologies has transformed the worlds of business and of decision making over the last 30 years. Artificial Intelligence (AI) will do so over the coming years too; albeit in markedly different ways, as digital is a world of exact science, whereas AI is a world of probabilities.

The algorithms that power digital technologies turn good data into good data while replacing human work. For example, when filling a tax return online, the tax authorities' algorithm takes all the data you input, and immediately calculates your tax liability, without the need for extra human work. Likewise, with self-scanning automated tills at the supermarket or corner shop. If the input data is not good the output data will be wrong (for example, if you misquote your salary on your tax return, hide a can from the till, etc.), but otherwise the output from the algorithm will always be correct.

With AI, in comparison, even good input data can lead to bad output data, because the output is generated statistically rather than mechanically. For example, an AI system specializing in lung cancer recognition on X-rays of lungs. The AI will have been 'trained' to recognize the presence of cancer by being fed thousands of X-rays where the answer (cancer or no cancer) is already known by the human handler. The first time the AI system is then presented with an image that hasn't been pre-diagnosed by humans, the answer it provides will only be true within the limits of statistical probability. The world of AI is a world of approximation, when the world of digital technologies is a world of certainties.

What does that mean for strategic thinking and complex business problem solving? It's too early to tell. One can still take away three truths worth pondering, regarding the dataset, the values set and the accountability of AI.

> **AI works on data from the past.** As we saw above, AI systems need to be trained on pre-existing data. The datasets used have typically been gathered over years or decades, and are subject to the prevailing biases of these times. It is well documented that early self-driving AI in cars had difficulty recognizing women, and people of colour. Because the AI had been trained to recognize people using millions of photos of white men. Not necessarily intentionally racist or misogynistic, just a reflection of the inventory of photos available at the time. Similarly, if you were to construct an AI system to help predict career success in an organization, it might suggest that being white, male and middle-aged are good predictors. Because it was historically true. The dataset itself is not in a position to spot *what data is missing* from the set; humans need to do that.

> **AI modelling is highly skewed by the values of the past and/or the values of its programmer.** We've seen how a dataset can be skewed. Sometimes even the thinking can be too. For example, a call centre manager might want to ensure that future recruits match the characteristics of strong perform-ing team members to date, and these may historically have been women of colour. (As was the case for NASA and its pool of 'human computers' in the 1970s, well documented in the 2016 film *Hidden Figures*.) Any AI sifting the CVs of candidates today might be skewed in reflecting the values of the past. Predictive texting in your mobile phone is another AI system that can reflect the values of its programmer. When someone types 'ducking' in their text box, what auto-correct suggestions does the programmer allow? None, the statistically most likely, or a prudish one? Many less visible examples of such skewed thinking hide in the folds of many an AI system, existing and coming soon.

> **AI accountability is unclear, between the manager and the machine.** Most banks will soon have AI systems that auto-matically approve loans, on the basis of numerous

characteristics analysed together to determine creditworthiness by applying statistical probability; a decision historically taken by bank managers. Should the loan perform badly, who should the bank's shareholders approach to complain? The bank manager, the programmer of the AI system, the AI system itself? Imagine now the same issue regarding the lung cancer case we saw. If you are the patient, declared cancer free by the AI, and then found a few years later to be riddled with cancer cells, with only a few months to live. Who do you sue: the doctor, the AI, the AI programmer, etc.?

It is still a bit too early to tell how the prevalence of AI will impact strategic thinking as a whole. AI systems are already used in the 'Down' part of the Rollercoaster of Strategic Thinking, to eliminate options. For example, a session of Mutation Game can quickly create several thousand possible alternative sentences, and a trained AI might help prioritize the hundred or so that are statistically most likely to prove useful. On the 'Up' part, we're still quite a long way off from AI systems generating creative options. Most are closer to a giant spelling auto-correct function than a 10x version of Leonardo da Vinci. The earliest impact might be on the 'Push' to Conviction element, where AI systems can help sieve through millions of social media posts to capture whether a recent new idea you've Lean tested out there is doing well, and should therefore be rolled out at scale.

In conclusion: say hi to AI. It will have an as yet unclear impact on the 'Down' and 'Push' parts of strategic thinking, and we should all stay abreast of developments.

12.

CONCLUSION

Strategy can be scary. All that future, all that unknown, all that risk. 'What's our current strategy on X?', 'Is my strategy working for Y?', 'Do we need a new strategy with Z?', etc.

Rather than obsess about strategy, this book has invited you to focus on strategic thinking. **Strategy as the output, strategic thinking as the method.** If you tackle a given problem in a highly strategic way, then the strategy that will result is highly likely to be much better. You'll know what to do next, with clarity, certainty and conviction.

We've seen that you and your team will typically need to think strategically about a particular issue you face if:

> - the problem is **big**
> - it lies in the **future**
> - it's **never been done** before
> - there will likely be **very little data**
> - the best answer is **not just a matter of taste**, and
> - it will **require proof** to convince many stakeholders.

Feedback nuggets

I've been helping over 10,000 people become more strategic in the last 20 years, via live training sessions, online courses, private coaching, global webinars, etc. As you can imagine, I have received a lot of feedback on what has worked and what didn't resonate for people. Sometimes immediately at the end of a session, sometimes after six months, sometimes 10 years later when a former participant becomes a client and invites me to come and train their new team. Many people I have approached with post-training surveys, others have come to me proactively to share two or three key memories they felt had been turning points in their professional careers (and often their personal lives too).

Allow me to outsource the conclusion of this book on *How to Be Strategic* to these former training participants. They have helped me develop the content you've found in the book, refine the anecdotes and case studies, and unearth the key learnings over time. Here are the eight most common nuggets of feedback that they consistently share with me.

1. **'Being strategic is good for your career'**
2. **'Being strategic is a mindset, not a toolset'**
3. **'The future can't be analysed; it can only be created'**
4. **'Strategic = Creative + Analytical'**
5. **'You don't need real data to have real ideas'**
6. **'You need real data to have real solutions'**
7. **'Tool X changed my life'**
8. **'The Up–Down–Push mantra really works'**

Let's unpack these nuggets in turn.

1. BEING STRATEGIC IS GOOD FOR YOUR CAREER

I get thanked a lot. By people who frequently mention that they first understood strategic thinking when we trained together. I know, and they know, that they could have understood it elsewhere first. Reading strategy books, doing an MBA, launching a startup, serving an apprenticeship to a very strategic boss, etc. We're not debating here whether my teaching is better than the other teaching they were exposed to – or could have been exposed to. Just that, years later, they could cast a sideways glance towards their peers, and notice that there was a common theme between those who were doing better and the others. A clear correlation between professional success and strategic-thinking skills.

The causality might be that more successful people became more strategic (because they had to, under the pressure of new responsibilities). The more likely causality goes the other way around: people who were better at handling strategic issues got recognized for this by their stakeholders (boss, clients, etc.) and were offered more responsibilities, leading to better and faster success. Startup founders who manage their limited cash more strategically go further too, and the same applies to freelancers and self-employed professionals. Being strategic is good for your career – whatever your career of choice.

2. BEING STRATEGIC IS A MINDSET, NOT A TOOLSET

Clients who hire me to train their team or their company often want a comprehensive list of the tools and techniques I'll be sharing with their people. Especially ahead of a first training session. Once this first session is finished, all the participants comment upon how, in just a few days, they acquired a radically different mindset, seeing solutions much faster and with much greater clarity. They realize that the mindset is key, and the toolset is somewhat incidental.

Clearly, the more tools you have in your toolkit the more complex strategic problems you can tackle. Practice does make perfect too – as it does in yoga, piano, chess, and most other forms of human activity. But there is something more important than how broad your toolkit is, and how lengthy your practice has been. In strategic thinking, as in many other fields of human activity, the moment of epiphany is when the penny drops, and you finally 'get' it. The mindset.

In the specific case of strategic thinking, the penny often drops when you realize that you need a different problem-solving route to arrive at convincing conclusions on complex problems. You fully embrace the truth that the path you take on garden variety day-to-day issues doesn't work for big problems. And that's because complex problems, strategic issues, exist mostly in the future – and the future is a different country.

3. THE FUTURE CAN'T BE ANALYSED; IT CAN ONLY BE CREATED

Most people spend most of their days at work in the Expert mode. Knowing their stuff, helping others, and being recognized as the person with the answer to everything in their field of expertise. That's because a lot of their work life is ruled by a specialist to-do list, in the present, and the fallout from the latest crisis, in the recent past.

I've trained all the business functions over the last 20 years. Strategy, marketing, finance, product management, IT, HR, sales, etc. More often than not, the people in the room with me have been very good at their job, exhibiting great enthusiasm, and a strong analytical disposition. It would commonly puzzle them that some categories of problems didn't yield to their favourite approach: large amounts of data, analysed with huge effort, by extremely bright people. You know now the simple answer: the future can't be analysed; it can only be created.

There is simply too much unstructured and unreliable data in the future for the answer to your current strategic conundrum to arrive through the simple application of brute analytical force to that mountain of hazy facts. Demographic evolution, societal changes, AI, robots, new specialist legislation, etc. Too many changes on the horizon. There is always a new trend around the corner that you won't have thought of. If you try to solve a complex problem through the accumulation of knowledge on these future trends, you will always feel that you are just one day of analysis short of the elusive perfect solution. Give me one more day and I'll be fine. One more glass of data. Like a data-holic. It never ends well.

It doesn't matter which industry you work in, or which function you occupy, your job won't be the same in two years. Because everything around you changes. It's unnerving, and it can make people restless. So many unknowns, so little time. The only thing that won't change is your ability to think through the implications of each of these new changes that the future holds in store for you, your team, your business, or your industry. You can't know the future, but you can structure your response to it, by first imagining a number of possible futures. How does one create these possible futures?

4. STRATEGIC = CREATIVE + ANALYTICAL

This insight can be read two ways. People with strong analytical skills need more creativity to become truly strategic. Conversely, people of a more creative disposition need to graft some analytical engine to their unbridled creativity to become more strategic.

This insight must also be read from left to right. To be strategic, first be creative, then be analytical. First create a range of possible futures, then analyse these various possible futures, to discover the best possible outcome.

Getting organizations to become more strategic usually means finding a way for the 'creative' types to work well with the 'analytical' types. Giving them a common vocabulary, mutually appreciating the key role played by the other, embracing the superior results that joint work delivers. And also emphasizing that different people should be steering things at different times. Creative comes first, analytical second. First create the futures, then analyse them.

Getting individuals to become more strategic is harder. Because it doesn't involve getting two existing tribes to play nicely with each other; it involves acknowledging in oneself that one of the skills may not be present at all yet. Helping highly 'creative' people here means helping them build their own analytical powers, when they may have spent the last 20 years being afraid of numbers and how maths made them feel so small at school. Similarly, helping highly 'analytical' people here means helping them build their own intuitive muscles, when they might be extremely uncomfortable with uncertainty and the subjective world of strong emotions.

Becoming more strategic as a person involves becoming more rounded as a human being. It is at least as much a personal self-development job (starting from within) as it is a professional development one (coming from a coach or trainer on the outside). Luckily, the techniques we've seen to go 'Up' to the point of Clarity can be mastered by anyone, whatever their background.

5. YOU DON'T NEED REAL DATA TO HAVE REAL IDEAS

A good idea may not be a rational idea. A good idea may even come from the most unlikely place. Children are commonly acknowledged to be highly creative. Yet children have barely any data worth mentioning. You don't need real data to have real ideas.

Analysing data is really good at making sense of the past, and not so great at making sense of the future. Because most forecasts will prove to be false. The majority of future data is as unreliable as your average long-range weather forecast.

Expertise is a great way to have ideas for solutions to problems. But it cuts two ways with brand-new issues. An expert has become an expert through learning and storing a huge amount of data in their field. They might know a shortcut to a great idea that others might miss. On the downside, experts have a way to freeze out or underestimate the contributions from others, however wonderful they might be. History is littered with the remnants of experts and incumbents who didn't see the winds of change.

Genius-level creativity is the third source of ideas that many people worship. Rightfully so. I've been lucky enough to see a few geniuses at work, and their ability to intuit options with little data and zero expertise can be awe inspiring. But it's rare, and can't be relied upon to show up when you need it most.

That's where the secret weapon comes in. Something that reliably helps you come up with unexpected ideas, early on projects, without much data, expertise or genius. That secret weapon is structure.

Pyramid Principle, **Happy Line** and **Mutation Game** are three brilliant structured thinking techniques that help a group of mixed-ability colleagues identify a broad range of ideas quickly, without much data or expertise required to contribute. You don't need real data to have real ideas when you have structure.

6. YOU NEED REAL DATA TO HAVE REAL SOLUTIONS

The business of business is to get things done and achieve satisfactory outcomes. 'Vision without execution is just hallucination', as Thomas Edison famously said. Mike Tyson expresses the same thing when he says that 'everybody has a plan until they get punched in the mouth'.

Many people love their ideas, their vision, their plan, so much that they would prefer to keep the dream alive rather than be proved wrong by reality. They want to convince others of the validity of their vision through lobbying and the force of their own personality. Startup founders, in particular, can display a strong sense of vision, and create a 'reality distortion field' around them. It can only work for so long – or in fields where subjectivity rules (mostly the arts and other purely creative pursuits). Like gravity, reality can only be denied for so long. It has a habit of laying waste to 'the best laid plans of mice and men', as Robert Burns would have it.

There are three quotes in the two paragraphs above, to reinforce the message that we are dealing with a universal truth. You may not need real data to have real ideas, but you do need real data to have real solutions. Because until it has been tested against the harsh light of reality, your idea is not yet a solution.

This particular truth is the one that many training participants mention took them the longest to embrace and own. They understood it in theory in the classroom, as you hopefully have when reading this book. But the only way to really get to the truth contained here is through failure. Abject failure, expensive failure, utterly unexpected failure. I've had a few. Only when a big and treasured plan fails, and you can still vividly remember how absolutely convinced you were that it would succeed, do you truly appreciate that you don't have a real solution until you have real data. So go and get some as quickly, cheaply and often as you can.

Payoff Profiles Matrix, **Landscape Analysis** and **Lean Startup** are three brilliant techniques to help you discover which one of your current ideas is the true gem. The one that can survive contact with reality. The one that will turn into a fantastic solution to your strategic issue over the next few days, months or years, for your business, your function, your team, or yourself.

7. TOOL X CHANGED MY LIFE

Each tool or technique we've seen in this book does a specific job. The Pyramid Principle is great at structuring a desirable end-point (and works best when you know what success you'd like). The Mutation Game, on the other hand, works best when you know you have a problem with your starting point, but have no clue on the end-point. People tend to respond really strongly to the tool that helps them best in their moment of need. You will profusely thank someone bringing you a spoon when looking at a bowl of soup with empty hands, and a knife offered at that point will leave you cold. Your enthusiasm is largely a function of your immediate need, not a reflection of something that is essentially better about any given tool.

I love each tool equally, because I know that every single one of them has transformed someone's life. We've seen 12 tools in this book (in addition to the Rollercoaster itself). You might have in mind two or three tools right now that you rate massively in excess of the others. I can guarantee you that I have had feedback from people praising these very tools as their favourites too.

Conversely, reread in a few months' time the chapters that you enjoyed the least – and you might discover that they contained nuggets all along. Your needs will have changed, and your appreciation too. Maybe one of the six techniques to help convince others will strike you as much better than you first remembered. Be it **NLP Language, 10 Ways to Convince, Memorable Metrics, Pocket NPV, Pyramid Principle** or **Adland Swagger**.

8. THE UP–DOWN–PUSH MANTRA REALLY WORKS

This is the reason why this book exists. I've lost count of how many times training participants told me they drew the shape of the Rollercoaster of Strategic Thinking for their team. Just back from a training session, that was the first thing they wanted to share with their colleagues, bosses and direct reports.

The contrast between the Strategic route and the three other routes to completion (Expert, Analytical, Creative) is something that everybody seemed to understand quickly and intuitively. It made sense, it felt right. More importantly, it proved true. Time and time again, they explained to me that they went back to the Up–Down–Push mantra whenever they were faced with difficult, strategic issues, and they could always find a way through, with one or more of the tools.

I hope you've enjoyed *How to Be Strategic*, and that it serves you well in your professional and personal development. Let me know how it goes on www.strategic.how when you have a minute. You've probably worked out by now that I thoroughly enjoy feedback, and I look forward to staying in touch.

Don't worry, be strategic!

ACKNOWLEDGEMENTS

I feel immensely grateful for the many people who have helped me give birth to *How to Be Strategic*.

First and foremost are the thousands of business consultants, corporate executives and tech startuppers who have been on the receiving end of my training. They have helped me discover new strategic concepts, select the best ones, refine my presentation skills, and validate applicability in the real world. Without their wonderful patience, enthusiastic support and sometimes blunt feedback, none of this book would have been possible. Thank you.

I have been grateful throughout my career to have mentors who have pushed me to accomplish more than I could have on my own. Jérôme Bédier, Franck Biancheri, Frédéric Faurennes and Richard Doherty took a chance on me when I was fresh out of rocket science school, and introduced me to the delights of consulting, lobbying, and public speaking to hundreds in large venues. Thank you for such a great start to a professional career.

Julian Vyner is responsible for both recruiting me into the high IQ world of consulting after INSEAD and, much later, for opening my mind and my heart to the EQ side of life. Clare Sillery and Jody Day have each contributed equally to my growth as a man on that front. For the past ten years Dominique Turcq has been a wonderful role model and sounding board from afar. Thank you all for presenting me with so much opportunity for growth.

Over twenty years of working with clients, all have been important, and some have been particularly meaningful. Backing a brand-new idea, opening the right door at the right moment, offering support, teaching me a lot. Amongst the many I'd like to thank are Toby Robinson, John

Petevinos, Chris Outram, Gill Whitehead, Luke Jensen, Jean-Michel Mollo and John Smith. Thank you – and to the many other clients not mentioned here.

In essence, I'm now an ideas retailer. Scanning the horizon for great new strategic ideas, trying them for size, embracing those that offer great rewards for the right amount of effort, and discarding the rest. I'd like to thank here the creators of the best ideas I work with: Barbara Minto, Chan Kim, Julian Vyner, Edd McLean and Eric Ries. Thank you.

As you can imagine, this book involved a tremendous amount of feedback, iteration and rewriting. I received invaluable feedback from Jacques Mulbert, Russell Davies, Marc de Speville, Birger Steen, John Smith, Dominique Turcq, Edd McLean and Ivan Mulcahy. Thank you for your suggestions, feedback and support.

At Penguin, my superb editor, Martina O'Sullivan, saw the vision of this book right away and enthusiastically guided it through the entire process. I want to also thank Shân Morley Jones, Emma Brown, Francisca Monteiro, and everyone else who worked on making this book a reality.

My adviser, partner and number one fan throughout the publishing process has been my phenomenal agent, Ivan Mulcahy. He has the amazing ability to find the right turn of phrase to charm an opening here, soothe an anxiety there and make things happen, whilst keeping everyone happy, all at once. Thank you, my friend.

Finally, I'd like to turn to the future and thank you, the reader, for picking up this book. I look forward to your feedback once you've read it and, more importantly, once you've applied the techniques in practice in your professional life. So, to you too, thank you!

INDEX

Page references in *italics* indicate images.